Modern Film Dramaturgy

Kerstin Stutterheim

Modern Film Dramaturgy

An Introduction

PETER LANG

**Bibliographic Information published by the
Deutsche Nationalbibliothek**
The Deutsche Nationalbibliothek lists this publication in the Deutsche
Nationalbibliografie; detailed bibliographic data is available online at
http://dnb.d-nb.de.

Library of Congress Cataloging-in-Publication Data
A CIP catalog record for this book has been applied for at the
Library of Congress.

Cover image: Jasper Stutterheim
Cover Design: © Olaf Gloeckler, Atelier Platen,
Friedberg

Printed by CPI books GmbH, Leck

ISBN 978-3-631-79650-4 (Print)
E-ISBN 978-3-631-79874-4 (E-PDF)
E-ISBN 978-3-631-79875-1 (EPUB)
E-ISBN 978-3-631-79876-8 (MOBI)
DOI 10.3726/b16012

© Peter Lang GmbH
Internationaler Verlag der Wissenschaften
Berlin 2019
All rights reserved.

Peter Lang – Berlin · Bern · Bruxelles · New York · Oxford · Warszawa · Wien

This publication has been peer reviewed.

www.peterlang.com

Whoever has read texts by Kerstin Stutterheim before, will know that her field of expertise is film dramaturgy. In this new book, Stutterheim returns to present the core of her research: highlighting the need to pay attention not only to the structure and the basic level of the narration of a film, but also to the audio-visual presentation of the stories - their aesthetic aspects - in order to understand the ultimate meaning of the film. *Modern Film Dramaturgy* is an inspiring and enriching text for film analysts and creators. Through sharp advice and practical examples, the author succeeds in whetting the appetite of the reader to learn more about the role that dramaturgical knowledge plays in the creative process of film production.

Prof. Carmen Sofia Brenes
School of Communication
Universidad de los Andes-Chile

To significant extents, *Modern Film Dramaturgy* by Kerstin Stutterheim has helped my drama students understand and strategically bridge the gap between the ideation and execution of the film. By the fourth week of a five-part lecture and workshop series based on explicit and implicit dramaturgy, the students evidence professional skills of crafting stories clearly reflecting socio-cultural, political contexts, as well as significant correspondences. They also showcase the ability to deploy audio-visual subtexts to showcase themes, as well as significant moments in the plot, like preludes and turning-points and endings. With the teaching on implicit dramaturgy, these students are learning to approach filmmaking with the consciousness that dramaturgy is the drawing board, which helps maintain the intricate elements of the directorial vision, throughout the three phases of production to arrive at "elegant" visual storytelling, which Stutterheim richly unpacks. In my practice as a screenwriter and director, the book has informed my need to closely involve a dramaturg in the developmental stages of my works. Directors keen on maintaining the super objectives of their films will find the book valuable; tutors will find it promptly supportive for guiding aspiring filmmakers.

Dr. Samantha Iwowo
Directing Drama for Film & TV
Bournemouth University

Foreword

Film theory, which is only a little younger than the film itself, aims at a better understanding of its aesthetics and cultural significance through the analysis of cinematic works. Film and cinematic narrative are part of many traditions, and film theory has developed a wide variety of approaches and film-scientific methods through which films are viewed. Many of the approaches feed on other theories: literary studies, art history, media philosophy, media studies, sociology, psychoanalysis or cognitive science. What is striking here is that in film studies, there seems to be the most considerable reluctance towards precisely the discipline that is closest to the art of cinematic storytelling: theatre studies. On the one hand, this reticence may be due to the focus on the semiotic-textual or the medial-formal; on the other hand, it may simply be due to the search for an academic territory of one's own - as in the case of a young person's cutting off the cord to his or her parents.

It is the merit of this book to show how deeply narrative film, in its way of narration, is connected with theatre - and this applies not only to classical, i.e. figure-centred and action-led storytelling in cinema but also to poetic, modern and postmodern narrative - be it in cinema, television or digital forms such as games and productions for the web.

As the author demonstrates, one can exemplify this deep rootedness by two facts: On the one hand, it is *the essence of the performative*, which is based on the performance characteristics of both art forms; on the other, it is the *dialectical essence of the drama itself*. The separation of the film from theatre began with the development of a specific film aesthetic - when the camera as a means of representation became an "organ" in its own right - but this does not change the fact that the structures of the cinematic narrative based on the traditional dramaturgy of the theatrical drama.

In this book, Kerstin Stutterheim raises a real treasure of theory. It advocates authors who are far too rarely taken into account by film studies and for concepts that are also little considered; and it makes these concepts productive for both contemporary film studies and film practice.

It thus becomes apparent that theatre dramaturgy, as a practical and theoretical discipline for film analysis, has more suitable concepts to offer than those borrowed from literary studies, for example. It illustrates in what diversity and in what detail dramaturgical models of narration and performance have already been considered in the history of theatre, and how this thinking was further developed into modern theatre dramaturgy in the 19th and 20th centuries. Moreover, the author shows that this thinking can help us today to analytically "come to terms" with the modern dramaturgies of the complex and metaphorically narrated films of the present.

I have personally experienced Kerstin Stutterheim's approach of using the terminology of traditional dramaturgy of the theatre to be very useful in my theoretical and practical work for film as well as in teaching. How Kerstin Stutterheim employs these concepts facilitates the description of a film's storytelling and a film's aesthetic, while at the same time triggering processes of fundamental perceptions and making them productive for your work. I have had positive feedback from students in academic courses as well as from prospective film authors that they have proved these concepts useful and applicable in practice.

The present book sheds light on European traditions of thought and knowledge from which modern film dramaturgy evolves - and which make the culture of screenplay guides re-imported from the USA to Europe appear like "old wine in new skins".

The author does solid groundwork here; with her well-founded specialist knowledge, she steps back, so to speak, a historical step behind the above-mentioned film-theoretical approaches and thus creates the necessary foundations, which have a deeper understanding of film as a prerequisite and allow it to succeed. The author introduces us to the insights of dramaturgy as a discipline that has much more to offer than explaining architectures and structures of closed dramatic narrative forms because dramaturgy is also a school of perception.

With the terms "open drama", "epic dramaturgy" and "implicit dramaturgy" derived from theatre dramaturgy, film narration can be precisely described and analysed with its aesthetic means. One can contextualise film-aesthetic phenomena through dramaturgical thinking – and strictly speaking, only this opens up a genuinely analytical-critical examination of the film.

Dramaturgy poses critical questions to its object, both in the conception of film art and in its reception and analysis: Why is something depicted precisely like this and not differently? What is the hidden meaning of what gets shown? The dramaturgical approach is holistic, focusing on both the aesthetics of reception and the aesthetics of production. With her dramaturgical view of film, the author thus succeeds in doing something that other approaches to film theory often fail to do: it is a genuine understanding of modern, post-modern and poetic film narrative. Therefore, this book is just as recommendable to all film scholars as it is to all film authors

Christine Lang, Berlin, July 2019

Contents

Preface

Movies, documentaries, TV series and games are part of our daily life in all its facets. Their structure, narrative techniques and conventions seem familiar and easy to understand. The tradition, which Jean-Claude Carrière once described as the "secret of narration", can be presented through methods of aesthetics of which dramaturgy is a sub-discipline. Dramaturgy as practice-based knowledge emerges from expertise and contextualisation. It facilitates creative practice, which in turn is permanent proof of its theory.

Dramaturgy is a profession and an academic discipline. As a practice, it is part of all narrative-performative arts. In academia, dramaturgy is a sub-discipline of aesthetics. Dramaturgy emerges from professional praxis and is dedicated to supporting performative-narrative artworks. Film dramaturgy evolves from classical dramaturgy known from theatre but specific to the medium.

Narrative-performative works – from theatre to movies and some games – follow dramaturgically identifiable conventions, which may vary in different regions and traditions. Through dramaturgy, one will be able to identify the pattern and its variations. Accordingly, the work of a dramaturg can vary or be differently defined depending on traditions within a particular region and production context of films and time-based narrative-preformative artwork.[1]

Notwithstanding local, historical or technical impacts, dramaturgy as a discipline contains conceptional knowledge of composition and structure of dramatic work, and aspects of its effect in the staging. One can call this comprehensive understanding of the poetic architecture of an artwork.[2] When explaining the inner systematics of philosophy, Immanuel Kant refers to the concept of structure as the architecture of pure reason.[3]

The definition used here is dramaturgy as the 'dialectic of performative arts'. The theory of dialectics is a form of thinking that is not content with

---

1   Cf. Romanska 2015; Turner & Behrndt 2016
2   Bachtin 1979, p. 106; Bachtin 2008a p. 36
3   Kant 1974, p. 15 et sequ.,

the conceptual order, but 'accomplishes a feat of correcting the conceptual order through the appearance of objects'.[4] In dialectical thinking, terms are continuously related to the processes or events to which they refer. This kind of reflection leads to changing definitional terms 'in a certain relation to the progress of thought, without, however, abandoning the determinations that the term originally had.'[5] That approach also applies to dramaturgy. Dramaturgical practice interrogates terms, categories, their meanings, and thus, the praxis gets continuously reviewed and renewed. Correspondingly, one cannot distinguish practice and theory from each other. Both should inform the expertise of a dramaturg.

Dramaturgical knowledge can be applied to all works regardless of their technical condition or execution. Even works, originated with no involvement of a dramaturg, follow a dramaturgy – which is applied consciously or unconsciously. Dramaturgical knowledge can bring stimuli as well as a certainty to creative artistic practice, mainly when used deliberately. However, a playwright, screenwriter or a director acting as dramaturg as well should consider environmental or situational aspects as well. For this reason, some vital differences distinguish film dramaturgy from theatre dramaturgy, in both the classical as well as the contemporary context.[6]

This book emerges from many years of experience in academia, higher education, and professional practice. It addresses students, scholars, colleagues, filmmakers and all professionals involved in making films, videos, audio-visual time-based media productions. It provides an introduction to modern film dramaturgy. It begins with a short introduction to the background of the discipline, how it emerged, and how it became established and how it is taught to the best of my knowledge. In the second chapter, the fundamental aspects of film dramaturgy and its basic rules get introduced. Chapter three discusses issues of peculiarities of modern dramaturgy, which is frequently referred to as the non-Aristotelian narrative. Also presented are distinctive features in the design of characters that differ from the classic heroic figure. It presents particularities of aesthetic design and thus of implicit dramaturgy. I will discuss the relationship between the

---

4   Adorno 2010, p. 18
5   Ibid.
6   Cf. Bordwell, Staiger, Thompson 2006, p. 17; Carrière 1999, p. 160

director, their artwork and the audience; and the concept of the cinema of meaning as well as the potential of arranging time and space chronologically or non-chronologically. In chapter four, a few patterns of modern dramaturgy get explained using several widely known and easy accessible movies as object of studies. Chapter five gives an overview of how modern film dramaturgy can be adapted for TV series. Opportunities and models will be discussed based on the above principles and selected examples.

This book draws on earlier texts on the topic, which were published in German as for example the *Handbuch Angewandter Dramaturgie* (Peter Lang Verlag 2015, 356 pages), *Handbuch der Filmdramaturgie* (2009 and 2011, Peter Lang) and *Game of Thrones sehen – Eine dramaturgische Studie einer TV Serie* (Fink Verlag, 2017).

Over the last two decades, I taught film dramaturgy at the Film University "Konrad Wolf" Babelsberg[7] and as a guest scholar at many other universities, such as the Aalto University Helsinki and the Universidade Federal da Bahia. I am regularly invited to give workshops on dramaturgy for filmmakers and professionals from a variety of disciplines. The present text has its roots in the study of dramaturgy at Deutsches Theater Berlin and the Humboldt University Berlin, Faculty of Philosophy II, and grows out of my experience as a dramaturg, author, filmmaker and lecturer over three decades. I have regularly published about film dramaturgy since 2010.[8]

Special thanks to Glenda Hambly, Sue Warren, Trevor Peters and Maike Helmers; I also want to thank James Fair, Gabbi Kalms, Peter Kalms, Maurice Michaels, and Tony Stoller for discussing the script and supporting me with their suggestions, as well as Kirsten Otto from the library of the Film University *Konrad Wolf* for her valuable support in securing specialised sources. And, last but not least, many thanks to my son Jasper Stutterheim, who supplied me with the graphs and the cover page to give my thoughts and concepts a visual expression. I want to thank my family and everyone who has stood by me during the time of writing this book.

---

7   Before it was known as HFF as well as Film Academy 'Konrad Wolf'
8   Cf. Stutterheim 2010, 2013b, 2013c, 2013d, 2014a, 2014b, 2017; Stutterheim & Lang 2013; Stutterheim & Kaiser 2011, etc.

A Short Backstory of the Dramaturg and Modern Dramaturgy

The Beginning

Although the study of technique and practice in drama and dramatic writing originated in Ancient Greece, dramaturgy as a discipline and practice began with the work of Gotthold Ephraim Lessing (1729–1781). Lessing was an author, philosopher and critic, best known for *Laocoon: or, The limits of Poetry and Painting* (1766),[9] *Minna von Barnhelm* (1763–67),[10] *Emilia Galotti* (1772),[11] and *Nathan the Wise* (1779).[12] Lessing was quite likely the first dramaturg ever appointed anywhere in the world. He served in this position at Hamburg's National Theatre, Europe's first permanent national theatre, from 1767–1770. One of his key responsibilities was to advise the theatre management and the creative team on how to attract an audience. Lessing analysed performance by concentrating, in particular, on the relationship between the quality of the playwright's work, it's staging, the actor's performance and the audience's response. Lessing's responsibility was to advise theatre productions from the planning stage through the rehearsal phase to their performance. The function of the dramaturg enabled Lessing to analyse and discuss why some performances were more successful than others. Inspecting and describing this precisely, he published a series of texts, which became known as *Hamburgische Dramaturgie* [*Hamburg Dramaturgy*] (1767–1769).[13] This collection of writings is, to my knowledge, the first book ever published on the subject of dramaturgy, which hence laid the foundation of its theory and practice.

To this day, the dramaturg, whether for theatre or film, gives the entire production cohesion. The dramaturgy provides production with a backbone. That applies regardless of whether it is theatre, performance or film.

---

9   Lessing 2012; Lessing & Frothingham, 1874
10 Lessing & Machaffie 1962; Lessing & Riemann, 1899
11 Lessing & Stahl 1946
12 Gotthold Ephraim Lessing 1868
13 Lessing & Berghahn 1981; Lessing & Zimmern 1962

Like Lessing, the dramaturg mediates between the text, the performance and the audience.

Establishing Period

Inspired by the concept of dramaturgy introduced by Lessing and propagated through his publications, a broad discourse about dramaturgical issues began.[14] Influential authors and philosophers, such as Johann Wolfgang von Goethe (1749–1832), Friedrich Hölderlin (1770–1843), Arthur Schopenhauer (1788–1860), Heinrich Heine (1797–1856), Georg Büchner (1813–1837), Richard Wagner (1813–1883) and Bertolt Brecht (1898–1956), to name a few, began to analyse their work as well as the work of others, employing Lessing's methodology.[15]

Today, a dramaturgical department is a vital part of every theatre. Most theatres, troupes or companies in Germany and central Europe have appointed dramaturgs either for one particular show, the 'production dramaturg'; and/or as a member of the dramaturgy department, where they are involved in strategic planning and collaboration with contemporary authors as well as overseeing or driving experiment and reform. As mentioned above, the work of a dramaturg can vary from place to place, from theatre to troupe and develops over time. However, there are constant, essential elements to their practice; they advise the board, support directors and their team, inform actresses and actors, edit programme information and answer audience questions. This practice comes into play in movie production as well. Film dramaturgy has a long tradition in Central and Eastern Europe as well as in Scandinavia. In the field of film, ideally, the dramaturg gets involved from the very first idea. Unlike a script doctor, the dramaturg dedicates herself to the entire production, not only to the written and spoken word, responds and supports all the arts and crafts involved. She makes sure that everyone is equally informed about the intention, the theme, the plot, the motivation of the characters, and all relevant elements.

In return, a dramaturg can ensure that there are neither redundancies nor gaps. For example, music should not also highlight aspects that are already

---

14 Hammer 1968, 1987
15 Büchner 1974

highlighted in the text or dialogue. On the other hand, the set designer can integrate elements that supplement what is said or the expression of the actresses, thus enriching the overall narrative. In the best scenario, the dramaturg advises the team until the premiere. Even with the editing, dramaturgical advice can have a positive influence on the final result (and save time). One can achieve coherence in the narrative with the help of continuous dramaturgical consultation.

Modern Film Dramaturgy Emerging

At the beginning of the 20th century, when the production of films began, the specific knowledge of theatre dramaturgy was adapted for the early cinema. That happened not only in Germany but also in continental Europe in general, the United States, the Soviet Union, Scandinavia, Latin America, and other regions. Moving images, not only movies, became an established form within the performing arts. The two decades following World War I are described as the time of 'movie-sation' of theatre and 'theatre-sation' of cinema.[16] Theatre and film intersected and cross-pollinated. The first film academy, The Gerasimov Institute of Cinematography, commonly known as VGIK, was founded in 1919 in Moscow. However, in Germany, creative cinema production began only late, nevertheless it became soon one of the most inspiring film nations – until the Nazi regime changed everything. 'Despite a few later successes, the German Cinema was never to know another flowering like this one, stimulated, as it was, on the one hand, by the theatre of Max Reinhardt, and on the other, by the Expressionist art (it is essential not to confuse these opposing styles).'[17] As Lotte Eisner has already emphasised, Max Reinhardt (1873–1943) must be the first to be named in the context of modern dramaturgy. Building on a successful career as an actor in Austria and Germany, he became director and owner of the *Deutsches Theater* (DT Berlin) in 1905. Reinhardt founded the *Kammerspiele* as an additional, smaller experimental theatre stage next to the DT. Expanding on this, he established a 'theatre-imperium' of several theatres, not only in Berlin but in other parts of Germany and Austria as

---

16 Cf. Fiebach 2015, pp. 346–352
17 Eisner 2008, p. 7/8

well, called the 'Reinhardt-theatres'. In the first half of the 20th century, the 'Reinhardt-theatres' were the most progressive and influential in Europe. Reinhardt became one of the most successful, admired, and inspiring directors of his time. Reinhardt also directed theatre and movie productions in the United States of America, as, for example, A MIDSUMMER NIGHT'S DREAM (Reinhardt, USA 1935) for which he applied his poetic theatre aesthetic as shown in figure 1 to figure 3 below.

Fig. 1–3: Max Reinhardt's MIDSUMMER NIGHT'S DREAM (USA 1935)

His artistic approach overcame naturalism. He founded a theatre that concentrates on people and at the same time reflects art and the world. Reinhardt pursued a pluralistic, playful approach. He wanted to celebrate stage art in all its diversity and variety; hence Reinhardt 'advocated pluralism: he wanted to celebrate the arts of the stage in all their variety and diversity.'[18] Reinhardt pioneered the switch from literature-based performance and theatre practice that was focused on delivering the spoken word to a 'chamber music of the theatre'; a theatre full of music, movement, and colour.[19] His unique style of direction provided the basis for an international revue-show-culture.[20] In his productions 'he adopted whatever style he deemed to be most appropriate to the given work and enlivened the text by liberally employing nonverbal elements like music, pantomime, expressive sets and colourful costumes.'[21] His objective throughout was to attract and entertain an audience.[22]

---

18 Malkin & Rokem 2010, p. 46
19 Fiebach 2015, p. 245/246
20 Ibid., p. 246
21 Malkin & Rokem 2010
22 Cf. Braulich 1983

Fig. 4: Alexander Moissi
as King Lear

Fig. 5: *Oedipus Rex*. Directed by Reinhardt

These two pictures (Fig. 4 and 5) may give an impression of Reinhardt's highly successful artistic approach at the time. It was not only as an actor/director but also as a theatre director that Reinhardt succeeded in bringing exciting artists and talents to his houses, which in turn enriched the artistic development. These include in particular his dramaturgs: From 1905 to 1932, Arthur Kahane, a writer and philosopher, was Max Reinhardt's permanent dramaturg at *Deutsches Theater*. Also, in 1922 and 1923, Reinhardt appointed two at that time young, provocative authors, Bertolt Brecht and Carl Zuckmayer, as dramaturgs. Brecht was just at the brink of his career as a playwright and director. His position as Reinhardt Dramaturg guaranteed him not only a steady income but also privileged access to the world of theatre, critique and editing. The same was true for Carl Zuckmeyer.

Reinhardt's revolutionary artistic approach met the Zeitgeist and the beginning of Modern Urbanity. The latter can be defined as a complex of new rhythms of life, of scientific and technological achievements that radically changed the world. In the second decade of the 20th century, cities grew, and the pace of life increased. Those involved in dramaturgy, aesthetic and film, reacted to the transformation occurring in daily experience and were forced to adapt to constant changes of perspective.[23] 'He had become

---

23 Fiebach 2015, pp. 248–258

so important that in solid middle-class families, everybody skipped the newspaper headlines to read Alfred Kerr's article on the previous night's performance. Berliners often went to the Reinhardt theatre several times a week, for the programme changed daily. When the cinema became an art-form, it quite naturally took advantage of Reinhardt's discoveries, using the chiaroscuro, the pools of light falling from a high window into a dark interior, which one was accustomed to seeing every evening at Deutsches Theater.'[24]

The young and rapidly growing film art of Central Europe adopted some of the techniques that Reinhardt developed and introduced for his productions. This trend also resulted from the fact that many of the actors who made their careers in Reinhardt's ensemble and the associated education, moved to the film.

The 1923 film DER STUDENT VON PRAG [THE STUDENT FROM PRAGUE] (Wegener and Rye, D 1913), for example, demonstrates the robust link between Reinhardt's theatre and the emerging cinema in Germany. Paul Wegener and others acting in DER STUDENT VON PRAG were members of Reinhardt's troupe. The aesthetic of that production and other films, as THE GOLEM (Wegener, D 1920), was also noticeably influenced by Reinhardt's directorial style.[25] Wegener directed THE GOLEM and acted the double-role of the main character and his shadow.

SUMURUN (Reinhardt, D 1910) demonstrates another aspect of Reinhardt's multiple influences on film history. *Sumurun* (Freska, o.J.) was Reinhardt's favourite pantomime – he first directed the theatrical version of it in 1909 at *Deutsches Theater*. In 1910, it became the first movie Reinhardt directed, and for this occasion, he established his own film company. Ten years later, when Ernst Lubitsch adapted *Sumurun* (Ernst Lubitsch, D 1920) as well, and Reinhardt's theatrical production had 'left his mark on Lubtisch's style.'[26] 'In SUMURUN (Lubitsch, D 1920) Lubitsch himself plays the hunchback, a tragic buffoon. When he transforms into a bizarre, disjointed, robot-like dance in which arms and legs seem to have a life of their own, it becomes evident that he was inspired by the stage version

---

24 Eisner 2008, p. 47
25 Ibid., p. 44, pp. 55–63
26 Ibid., p. 86

Fig. 6: SUMURUN. P. Negri and   Fig. 7: SUMURUN. Postcard
E. Lubitsch

of the famous pantomime. Wherever this light rhythm comes through, so rare in a German film, it is to Reinhardt that we should render homage. A few passages in SUMURUN foreshadow the elegance of the Americanized Lubitsch. (...) The American musical was to pattern itself on these delicate arabesques.'[27]

Lubitsch started his film career in Reinhardt's acting classes, as did Friedrich Wilhelm Murnau[28], to mention another well-known and influential movie director. Lubitsch joined the DT Berlin in 1911 and was soon performing in films too. By 1915, he had graduated to directing. Lubitsch also plays a role of interest and influence in the evolving history of dramaturgy in theatre and film. He often took classic drama subjects or plots and deconstructed them, reorienting this tradition of drama narration to the point of view of the common people. He adapted familiar musical theatre or operetta techniques, which allow characters to step out of their role and comment on the action, and sometimes Reinhardt integrated new scenes providing a different perspective on well-known events.[29]

One can recognise traces of Reinhardt's influence over many years, as, for example, still in NINOTCHKA (Lubitsch, USA 1939). In this film act

---

27 Eisner 2008, p. 86
28 F.W. Murnau was one of the most influential directors of the 1920s, in particular within German Expressionism, e.g. NOSFERATU (Friedrich Wilhelm Murnau, D 1922). He migrated 1926 to the USA where he joined Fox Studios and produced three more movies in Hollywood, e.g. SUNRISE (Friedrich Wilhelm Murnau, USA 1927) until his death resulting from a car accident whilst filming TABU (F. W. Murnau, USA 1931)
29 Cf. Elsaesser 2000, p. 209/210

the former stars from Reinhardt's Deutsches Theater Alexander Granach as Kamerad Kopalski and Felix Bressart as Kamerad Bujanoff act in this film. Both had to flee from National Socialist Germany and started again in Hollywood, with Reinhardt-disciple Lubitsch as director.

Another influential figure for the development of modern theatre and dramaturgy as well as merging theatre and film is Erwin Piscator (1893–1966). Piscator founded the Proletarian Theatre in Berlin in 1920. A few years later he was appointed the director of Volksbühne Berlin. He formed a collaboration with dramaturg Felix Gasbarra (1895–1985), a German-Italian writer and journalist, aiming to establish a new political theatre. Piscator developed an aesthetic of epic storytelling for his performances, which enabled him to reflect on complex international socio-political processes. He believed theatre should depict socio-economic structures, their mechanism and movements and expose their character. Theatre, for him, was a political instrument with the potential to inspire and influence the audience. From his dramaturgical view, the figure on stage is not a tragic individual case but instead representative of its group. The main characters stand for the era and conditions of life. Piscator transposed this particular approach to his theatre productions by including projections of documentary film sequences, drawings, photographs, posters and other visual material.[30]

After immigrating to the United States in 1940 via the Soviet Union and France, Piscator became the director of the Dramatic Workshop of the New School of Social Research in New York in 1947. Harry Belafonte, Tony Curtis, Marlon Brando, Walter Matthau, Rod Steiger, and Tennessee Williams were among his students. Teachers at the New School under Piscator's stewardship included Stella Adler, Lee Strasberg, Hanns Eisler, Carl Zuckmayer, and Horst Pinthus, to name just a few.

In the 1920's the concept of 'absolute film' evolved from Modern Urbanism and constructivism, inspiring amongst others Viking Eggeling's SYMPHONIE DIAGONALE (Eggeling, D 1924) and Walter Ruttmann's OPUS-Series (D 1921–1925). From the artistic search for new aesthetic possibilities, the principles that define the 'absolute film' emerged. The artists interested in a modern, poetic film wanted to avoid a causal narrative;

---

30 Brecht 1967, p. 139; Fiebach 2015, p. 310; Müller 1927; cf. Willett 1978, pp. 58–61

they neither wished to educate the audience nor to convey experiences. Their interest was in rhythm and abstraction. Others artists of that period merged artistic approaches known from the stage, film, light, technological experiments and performances. For example, avant-garde artists, such as Ludwig Hirschfeld-Mack[31] and Laszlo Moholy-Nagy[32] experimented with light and film.[33]

Limited space and the aim of this book to focus on modern film dramaturgy has allowed only the briefest overview of how the arts merged into the Modern World establishing a 'new drama'[34], which in turn came to shape Modern Film Dramaturgy.

Teaching Modern Dramaturgy for Film

Besides practice, education and teaching also influence the establishment and development of dramaturgical practice and theory. Therefore a brief overview of how the tradition evolved in this area will be given below.

To my knowledge, one of the most influential figures in developing pedagogy for modern dramaturgy was Max Herrmann. Herrmann began as a Professor at Humboldt University in 1902 and founded the Theaterwissenschaftliches Institut [Theatrical-Scientific Institute] in 1923. His outstanding achievement was to change the approach to narrative-performative arts within the academia to a more 'philological exactitude: the facts must be ascertained before synthesis can be made or even a pragmatic nexus established. Max Herrmann insisted that a method must be developed that would allow for a scientific approach to theatrical facts.'[35] Herrmann's approach can be understood as a response to the historical context previously described: the influence of modern urbanism, the merging of theatre and film, a vibrant cultural explosion reacting on World War I, and the flowering of capitalism and consumerism. The core of Herrmann's pedagogical approach drew on the sensual aspect of narrative-performative artwork, inspired by Erwin Piscator and Max Reinhardt. When theatre studies

---

31 Hapkemeyer & Hirschfeld-Mack 2000, pp. 94–109; Hirschfeld-Mack 1923
32 Laszlo Moholy-Nagy 1967; László Moholy-Nagy 1925
33 Richter 2008; Janser, Rüegg, Richter, & Richter, 2001
34 Rühle 1988, p. 16/17
35 Nagler 1959, p. xxii

were still situated within the departments of Literature, German or English Studies, it was assumed that every aspect of a narrative-performative work depended on written and spoken dialogue. Herrmann changed that. 'The meaning of the verbal text is unchanged, but it ceases to be the only one. The theatrical performance is the played version of the text of a play.'[36]

One can still recognise the nature of theatre and theatricality in audio-visual works, even if one changes the technical medium. Symbolic action [*symbolisches Handeln*], as it is central in the dramatic narrative, is still visible movement in a film. Communicative practice and human creativity in the motion get presented through a theatrical presentation, understood as *Mimesis*. Dramatic art is always the core of performances and thus a symbolic act, be it on a stage or observed in public, politics, or a media production. Using technological channels does not take the dramatic moment away from any representation of human beings. Watching humans may be the primary source of aesthetic pleasure.[37] Thus, theatre studies are a valuable starting ground for analysing all performative arts. What is defined as 'theatrical' can be recognised in human culture of all times, around the world,[38] and in particular in contemporary media productions[39] as well as political or ideological performances of any kind.

Herrmann and his successors were convinced that it is not possible to teach the performative arts from texts alone. Thus, the experience of practice became an integral part of the concept of teaching both the performative arts and in theatre studies. The latter was understood to be the study of performative arts involving mimesis. Consequently, Herrmann's Institute not only cooperated with theatres to enhance the experience of their students, but the Institute also had a stage where students could, and were expected to, experiment.

Early cinema production, not only in Germany but in continental Europe (France and Poland for example), the United States, the Soviet Union, Scandinavia, Latin America, and other regions, drew on this tradition of theatre dramaturgy. Thus, with the film industry emerging, first

---

36 Nagler 1959, p. xxi
37 Fiebach 2006, p. 105
38 Cf. Schechner 1988; Fiebach, 2015; E. Fischer-Lichte 2013;
39 Fiebach 2002, pp. 17–41

'how-to'-manuals were written and published. Some of the authors offered courses or opened private schools.[40] The first academic approach, as well as artistic concepts of film dramaturgy, were discussed and published in the former Soviet Union.[41] And, as far as I can ascertain, the first book on dramaturgy for the film was released in Budapest in 1925: *A filmjáték esztétikája és dramaturgiája [Aesthetics and Dramaturgy of the Film Play]*[42] by Iván Hevesy. Hevesy was a film critic and playwright who taught film dramaturgy at film director Bela Gaal's private school in Budapest. 'Hevesy's approach is an original mix of theory and practice: he applies to the new art form the theoretical apparatus he acquired during his studies and that he had already applied in writing on art history, literary and art criticism, and music. As to practice, Hevesy had a keen sense for the technical aspects of filmmaking of the day.'[43]

As mentioned above, the first film school VGIK was established in Moscow in 1919. In 1929, Sergei Eisenstein, who taught at the VGIK amongst other well-known directors[44], published his text about the *dramaturgy of film form*[45] as a study of the dialectics of the style of film in which he also introduced the concept of a visual counterpoint as a cinematic form of conflict.[46]

Another influential book on film dramaturgy, Драматургия Кино *[Dramaturgy of the Cinema]* by V. K. Turkin, was published in 1938 in Moscow,[47] which was of not to be underestimated influence within eastern and central Europe. Many filmmakers and scholars from Europe, China, some other Asian and African countries, as well as few from the USA, studied in Moscow. Thus, they may have become familiar with Turkin's book as well. It was followed and referred to by Freilich's Драматургия Экрана *[Film Dramaturgy]*[48] and Ilja Waisfeld's Мастерство Кинодраматургия

---

40 Cf. Bailey 2014
41 Cf. Beilenhoff 2005; Tynjanov 1927
42 Hevesy 1925
43 Szekfü 2018
44 Cf. Gusner 2018
45 Eisenstein 1951
46 Ibid.
47 ТУРКИН/Turkin (1938) 2007
48 Freilich 1964

[Dramaturgy of the Movies][49] – both translated and published in German. Thought was dramaturgy as well by Mikhail Romm[50] and others at the VGIK, hence inspiring and influencing students from all over the world.[51]

The publication most influential, particularly in Hollywood since its early times, was Gustav Freytag's *Die Technik des Dramas* as *The Technique of the Drama*.[52] Freytag's approach influenced and still influences Hollywood's adaptation of the interpretation of Aristotle's analysis of the hero-driven, linear-causal, and action-based tragedy.[53] Aristotle's theories were forgotten for centuries but rediscovered during the 16th century, then newly interpreted and rewritten[54] by Francisco Robitelli, Arnold Hauser, Philip Sidney, and Julius Caesar Scaliger in particular.[55] These theories and publications gave the blueprint for a 'poetic of rules' and a 'poetic of imitation'[56] often referred to as introduced by Aristotle. These rules were declared as generally true and often presented as having been given since Ancient Greece. However, these conventions were developed in the early Renaissance in the context of the establishing of theatre buildings and closed stages. For example, Robitelli, Castelvetro, and Scaliger dogmatised that the action has to happen between sunrise and dawn[57] or less, thus shortening Aristotle's suggested time frame of one course of the sun,[58] and declared it a rule. Scaliger also enacted that the drama has to have three parts, and established the rules the Western Theatre followed[59] and still does. This sequence in theatre theory gave the background for Lessing's *Hamburgische Dramaturgie* as well as Freytag's *Technique of the Drama*. Layo Egri also refers to Freytag in *The Art of Dramatic Writing*.[60] Nonetheless, Egri expanded and shifted the focus of

---

49 Waisfeld 1966
50 Romm 1980; Romm 1974; M. I. Romm 1980
51 Gusner 2018
52 Freytag n.y.
53 Cf. Aristoteles & Schmitt 2008, Aristotle & Lucas 1968; Stutterheim 2015, pp. 107–113;
54 Benjamin 2011, p. 241
55 Fiebach 2015, pp. 106–109
56 Cf. G. Potter 2015, 2016, p. 360, Schmitt 2008b, p. X/XI
57 Carlson 1984, pp. 38–40; Spingarn 1899
58 Aristoteles & Schmitt 2008, chapter 5, b10–b15
59 Scaliger, Deitz, & Vogt-Spira, p. 29 et sequ.; cf. Spingarn 1899, pp. 40–50
60 Egri 2004

the argument to psychological elements and corresponding character traits. These two publications were of strong influence to the Hollywood tradition of a hegemonic understanding of dramatic narration and its structure.[61] Their approach to dramatic writing also led to a 'theory of moral world order'[62] within American film narratives.

After World War II, film dramaturgy continued and developed further as an established discipline in the Eastern hemisphere. It was and still gets taught at film academies in Moscow, Lodz, Prague, Bratislava, Berlin and Potsdam, as well as Beijing, and more, and more, in Scandinavia. The (rejuvenated) Institute of Theatre-Science at Humboldt-University also promoted the discourse of dramaturgy by employing the theories of Herrmann and Brecht and by establishing relationships internationally with academic institutions, researchers and theatres. Jean-Claude Carrière[63] founded the study of dramaturgy at the National French Film Academy *La Fémis*[64] in Paris when he became its founding director in 1986. In recent years, interest in film dramaturgy has grown in other parts of the world, although it has been almost exclusively based on the Western interpretations of Aristotle's *Poetics* and Freytag's corresponding writing, as previously outlined. The myth-based tragedy, on which both texts concentrate in particular, is derived from the original myths, which tells of the journeys of a hero.[65]

---

61 Cf. Stutterheim 2015, pp. 103–114
62 Cf. Benjamin 1991b
63 French novelist, screenwriter, actor, and founder president of *La Femis*, the French state film school. He collaborated with Buñuel, Peter Brook, Volker Schlöndorff, Umberto Eco, Michael Haneke and more. Carrière was conferred with an Academy Award (Oscar) for lifetime achievement in 2014, and more.
64 *La Fémis* is the most important national Film School in France
65 Cf. Thomson 1950

Dramaturgy as Discipline and Practice

A Solid Foundation from the Outset

> 'The notion and motion of action *are the locus
> and focus of dramaturgical thinking and doing in
> theatre, but also in cultural performances altogether.
> In varying degrees* action *is implied in all the other
> manifestations and comprehensions of dramaturgy,
> such as the composition, construction, strategy,
> devising, mediation, moderation, collaboration,
> feedback etc.*'[66]

One of the core elements of the concept of dramaturgy is the principle of a balance between constant and variable components. Constant features provide stability and are relatively easily recognisable – for creators and audience alike. These relate to our human experience of a reality, which is shaped by our perception as well as cultural memory.[67] Experiencing an event as it happens always differs from its representation, and that's why a film is an organised abstraction of reality – even if it is 'based on a true story'.[68] The process of abstraction incorporates dramaturgical patterns. Within aesthetics as well as psychology, it is acknowledged that pleasure often arises from the combination of the familiar with the surprising[69] – hence, it is one of the fundamental principles within dramaturgy. Intertwining the familiar with the surprising emulates the concept of constant and variable components. Constant features give the impression of coherence because they stabilise and, at the same time, facilitate a multitude of possible variations. They also play a significant role in explicit dramaturgy. Variable components also derived from tradition. Corresponding to the theme, the story, and the chosen form, one can determine flexible or variable factors to support narrative and action. Such a well-composed dramaturgical construction offers a refreshing new approach or provides an unexpected twist

---

66 Blažević 2016, p. 330
67 Cf. A. Assmann 2010, 2011; J. Assmann 2002
68 Carrière 1999, p. 133
69 Cf. Kahneman 2012

to a familiar story. A well-constructed balance of constant and variable elements allows us to adopt a particular rhythm as well as to develop the details of the respective narrative. The concept of variable and constant features has its roots in the dramaturgy of the theatre. The combination of these two elements serves structures that are inherent in human communication. In modern film dramaturgy, constant elements can be organised flexibly within the narrative up to a point. We use them to create the basis and the skeleton of a cinematic story.

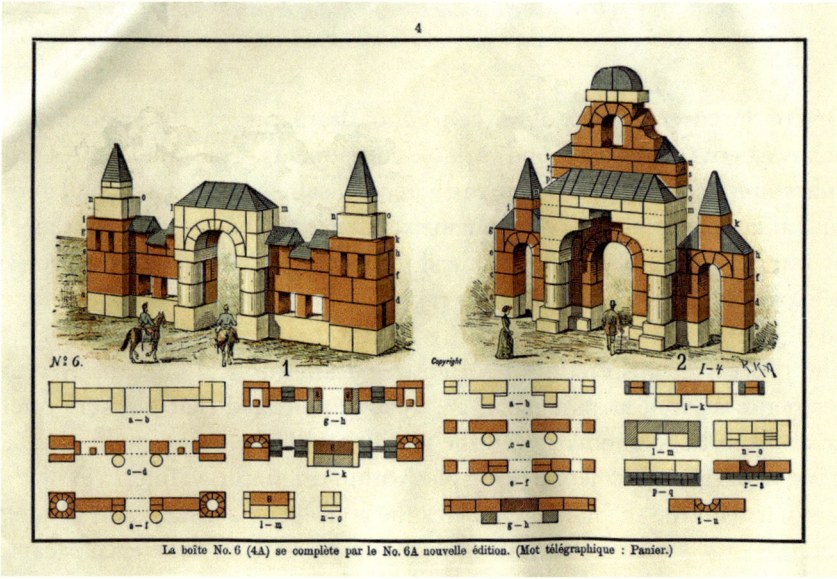

Fig. 8: Building Block Kit

One could compare dramaturgy with using a set of building blocks (as shown in Fig. 8) – one has to develop a foundation, which gives stability. Having done so, one can use the various building blocks to design the individual project one wants to achieve. There is no need to use every available element. Those in use can be arranged differently to give the work an attractive individual character. Variation leads to a distinct mode of expression. Another metaphor, which might help to provide an understanding of the matter, is that of the beauty of nature: everyone can recognise a species, such as a birch or a dog, through specific characteristics that apply to all individual plants or animals of this species. Nevertheless, each tree is different from the other, and the variation of the general characteristics gives the impression of the beauty of nature. This principle also applies to artistic works.

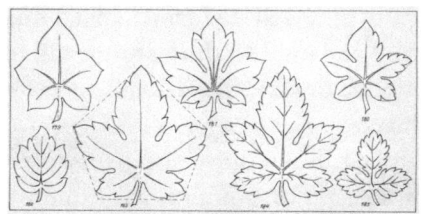

Fig. 9: Symmetry in Nature. By Th. A. Willig

Fig. 10: Constants and Variables in Nature.

Starting from this stable foundation of explicit dramaturgy, a filmmaker/writer/director can develop their creativity. This dramaturgical understanding enables the adoption of other dramatic modules and accordingly reveals the story depending on the subject and chosen form. Therefore, one speaks of explicit and implicit dramaturgy, which should be kept in balance with each other. These two aspects one can compare to 'slow and fast thinking',[70] which they also address. Daniel Kahneman, who was awarded the Nobel Prize for Economics for his work, defines human thinking as based on two interconnected systems. 'System 1', the 'automatic system', is the site of fast and associative thinking. 'System 2' is the 'effortful system', involves slower reactions.

> System 1 and 2 are both active whenever we are awake. System 1 runs automatically and System 2 is normally in a comfortable low-effort-mode, in which only a fraction of its capacity is engaged. (...) When system 1 runs into difficulty, it calls on System 2 to support more detailed and specific processing that may solve the problem of the moment. System 2 is mobilized when a question arises for which System 1 does not offer an answer (...). You can also feel a surge of conscious

---

70 Kahneman 2012

attention when an event is detected that violates the model of the world that System 1 maintains. In that world, lamps do not jump, cats do not bark, and gorillas do not cross basketball courts.[71]

Dramaturgy serves both systems: explicit dramaturgy represents the structural aspect of the narration and gets intertwined with the implicit dramaturgy that arouses associations and spontaneous reactions. Explicit dramaturgy ensures System 2 to be comfortable in its low-effort mode while System 1 feels entertained and happily busy by a well-designed implicit dramaturgy. In the following chapter, explicit and implicit dramaturgy will be explored in more detail. Explicit and implicit dramaturgy also relate to the principle of constant and variable elements.

One can compare the concept of explicit dramaturgy and its moment of familiarity with the architecture of a castle or a house, for example. Everyone knows that such a building has an internal structure. Although this inner structure is not visible to the eye from the outside, everyone understands that this construction has been built in a way that enables us to enter the building and move around without the house collapsing on top of us. The architectural design attracts our interest – as with the post-Victorian decorations of High Cliff Castle (Fig. 11) or the distinctive clarity in the design of the Bauhaus building (Fig. 12).

Fig. 11: High Cliff Castle   Fig. 12: Bauhaus Building

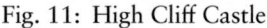

71 Kahneman 2012, p. 4/5

A modern film requires a reference to a familiar dramaturgical model to create a new artwork based on a stable foundation. Jean-Claude Carrière, who wrote LA VOIE LACTÉE [THE MILKY WAY] (Buñuel, F/I 1969) together with Luis Buñuel, can be cited in this context. Carrière describes that they wanted to throw all the established rules overboard for this film. They aimed to produce the most modern film of their time. After a few experimental attempts, however, it became clear to them that disregarding the "secret order" of a movie would only lead to frustration - both for the authors and for the audience.[72] Consequently, they developed a familiar dramaturgical structure as a foundation to evolve a nevertheless surprising and most modern movie.

Explicit Dramaturgy

The backbone of a film, no matter how conventional or experimental, is its explicit dramaturgy. Explicit dramaturgy primarily refers to aspects of the structure and the main level of narration of a film. It is defined as the 'architecture',[73] also known as 'story arc', plot, or 'story causality', or 'compositional motivation' or, to go with the Aristotelian term, 'generic motivation'.[74] A screenplay or original text, from which a director and producer(s) usually begin their work, already has a structure. It has a rhythm, a theme, and hence meaning, as well as the further potential for interpretation.

> A second skill film dramaturgy employs is the ability to find and help create structure. Film directors need pattern recognition, structuring, and story-shaping skills in order to make shooting and editing choices. These skills are essential because of the footage captured, even in fiction film, rarely conforms precisely to what the screenwriter wrote or imagined, yet it must be shot, cut, and re-arranged in an artful way. The dramaturgy of editing, in particular, is rarely appreciated by the general public, but, as Orson Welles observed, 'the whole eloquence of cinema is that it's achieved in the editing room.'[75]

Dramaturgy comprises the whole work, the complete action, as presented to an audience. As mentioned above, in explicit dramaturgy constant

---

72 Carrière & Bonitzer 1999, p. 207
73 Bachtin 2008a, p. 36
74 Aristoteles & Schmitt 2008, chapter 5, b10–b15
75 G. Potter 2015, 2016, p. 360 who quotes Welles from: Ondaatje & Murch 2002

elements are of crucial importance. They facilitate familiarity. One can recognise this effect in correspondence with slow and effortful thinking. The aspect of familiarity helps to invite the audience into a story, even though they are entering a new cosmos different from the world that the audience experiences in everyday life. To achieve this, one can start with a situation nearly everyone in the audience is acquainted with, such as singing, travelling through a landscape or having something to eat or drink.

One can also achieve an impression of familiarity by designing a structure, which responses to well- genre conventions, as in TRUE GRIT (Coen and Coen, USA 2010), THE PREPOSITION (Hillcoat, AUS 2005) or THE TRACKER (de Heer, AUS 2002). These directors use the genre convention for clarity of structure and to achieve the essence of familiarity. However, the stories of these three westerns are atypical of the genre. TRUE GRIT by being an adaptation of a movie made in 1969 featuring John Wayne, which was an adaption of a popular novel,[76] can rely on the conventions and the memory of the members of the audience and tells a well-known story in a new aesthetic, hence giving it a new meaning. THE TRACKER also uses the conventions to present a well-known story from a new perspective. The film begins with a typical Western situation. A group of men must ride into the wilderness to capture an Aboriginal man accused of raping a white woman. This setting is reminiscent of Western genre conventions as well as reflecting postcolonial stereotypes. The whites can only find this man with the help of a local tracker. From this constellation, two protagonist-versus-antagonist levels were created that were placed in relation to each other: A conflict constellation emerges, pitting the group against the Aborigine fugitive, as well as from the antagonistic relationship between the whites and their Aboriginal tracker. The theme running through the entire plot is a reflection on the violence of the white colonialists against the Aborigines. Every image, dialogue and gestus expresses this theme.

Gestus is defined as the way of expressing meaning and social-historical context through acting and hence is more than a gesture.[77] The use of

---

76 Portis 1968

77 Gesture is a term traditionally used in German theatre, although it became associated with Brecht who refined the definition and insisted that a gesture is not just expression but a social-historical significant pantomimic. Cf. Kuba 2005

genre conventions and constant dramaturgical elements allow us to tell a known story from a new perspective and therefore to present the story as an untypical, poetic, and an ironic counterpart to, for example, a Hollywood Western.

Even if one wants to create an unusual story or a movie playing with conventions, one can create the moment of familiarity with a simple means: in the exposition, the figures are allowed to do something, which the audience can relate to their everyday experience. A character can make a cup of tea or coffee or drink it, for example. Waking up and travelling are also familiar moments.

An example may illustrate this: the first scene of a movie, which opens with a couple sleeping. An inserted title heads 'Monday'. The man wakes up, grabs his watch, which shows the time as 6:12 a.m., and he slips the watch over his wrist. He kisses his wife, and they chat, he gets up, makes breakfast. A matchbox lies on the table, which he picks up and observes. He leaves for work. So far, it seems to be a typical Monday morning introducing the audience to a couple who all of us can understand and connect with. On his walk to work, he starts to compose a poem about the matchbox we have seen beforehand. Until now, the story seems to be close to everyday life experience for most of the members of the audience. The situation in which this man starts to compose a poem is not too surprising, although perhaps unexpected. By beginning PATERSON (Jarmusch, USA/F/G 2016) in the way described above, Jarmusch ushers the audience into a poetic movie about poetry. When combining poetry with a young bus driver's everyday life, it becomes accessible to the audience. Paterson as bus driving poet connects 'high art' with everyday situations. When establishing the main character as someone who represents the poet and the rhythm of poetry, Jarmusch can change the tempo as well as the representation of the narrated reality throughout the movie. Real time becomes more and more relative and events the poet observes while driving are more related to his poetry than the real world.

When designing the explicit dramaturgy for a film, one has to decide and develop a particular structure that best fits the story to be told, which involves constant and variable elements. *Chronotopos*[78] is a term defining

---

78 Bachtin 2008b

the relationship of time and space within a narrative. A central requirement in designing explicit dramaturgy is the choice of a structure and specific chronology, to set up a Chronotopos in which to position the characters. Structure and chronotopos are interconnected. They determine how all action is constructed. The parameters of this dramaturgical system govern the narrative, character(s), and the action. These elements define relationships within the story, the particular chronology as well as the rhythm and pace of the film narration.

At the beginning of the exposition, one should create a situation through which one can establish the theme and action, the aesthetic approach, place and time as well as the main character(s). This includes the already mentioned chronotopos as time-space-construction and reference to a genre.

Plot and story are terms within literature and film studies. In Russian literature, *sujet* and *fabula* are terms defining fundamental aspects of a film.[79] Through its adaptation into Anglo-American film studies, the sujet becomes story, and fabula turns into plot.[80] In dramaturgical terms, sujet/story comply with explicit dramaturgy, fabula/plot with the theme, which are reflected through implicit dramaturgy. 'Plot is not a story or a narrative but rather a dramaturgical scaffolding that arranges the order of story-telling incidents in an order that culminates in cathartic release. In this (…) model, the dramaturg concerns him- or herself foremost with the plot, the arrangements of incidents – in other words, with dramatic structure.'[81]

More constant elements in explicit dramaturgy, as the introduction of the protagonist(s) and other characters, and the moment that triggers the action will be discussed in more detail in the following chapters and explored with selected examples. It must be emphasised here: characters always serve the action: Characters are created, designed, interpreted and performed; characters by themselves are incapable of deciding anything for themselves in their own right.

As one of the variable elements, a *prelude* can be situated at the very first part of a film. In dramaturgy, one understands a 'prelude' to be a short sequence before the exposition starts, in a segment situated before

79 Lotman, 1981b; Sklovskij 2005; Tynjanov 2005
80 Cf. Bordwell et al. 2006, p. 12/13
81 Romanska 2016, p. 1

the title(es). This resembles the prologue as known from theatre and can tell a backstory — for example in Au Revoir Les Enfants (Malle, F/D/I 1987) where the mother bits farewell her son before he has to leave Paris; or to introduce Daniel Craig as the new James Bond in Casino Royale (Campbell, UK/CS/USA/D/BHA 2006). For Fly Away Home (Ballard, USA/CDN 1996), the prelude shows the accident in which the film's main character Amy (Anna Paquin) is injured and her the mother gets killed. After the titles, the story begins with Amy moving from New Zealand to Ontario in Canada and to start a new life.

Hitchcock and Lean, on the other hand, attuned their audience by using a musical overture before the film begins. For Spellbound (Hitchcock, USA 1945) the overture lasts six minutes, and for Dr Zhivago (Lean, UK 1965) a picture of a birch grove holds a fifteen-minute long prelude.

The Construction Principle

Gustav Freytag illustrated the construction principles of a drama with a triangle, as shown in figure 13. This model still serves today as the basis for demonstrating the dramatic structure.

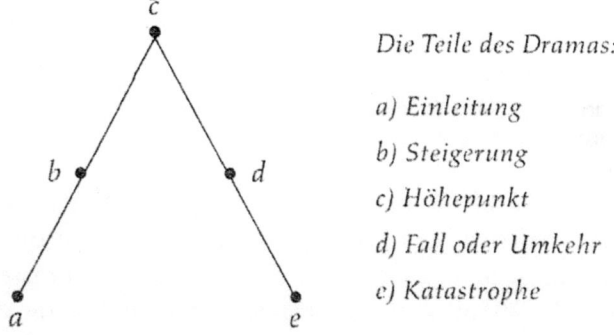

Die Teile des Dramas:

a) *Einleitung*

b) *Steigerung*

c) *Höhepunkt*

d) *Fall oder Umkehr*

e) *Katastrophe*

Fig. 13: Gustav Freytag – The parts of the drama: a) exposition b) increase c) climax d) reversal e) catastrophe

The graphic below (Fig 14) presents an enhanced understanding of the construction scheme of explicit dramaturgy for the classical, closed, linear-causal structure driven by a central character. For modern film dramaturgy, the graphic changes according to the other dramaturgical rules, as explained above.

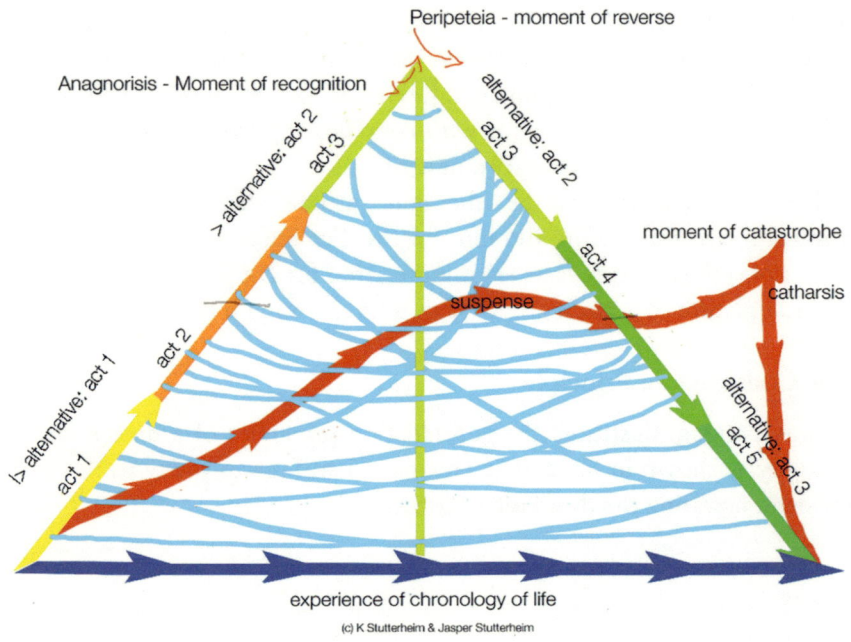

Fig. 14: Construction Scheme of a Drama of the 'Closed Form'
© Kerstin Stutterheim & Jasper Stutterheim

The bottom line of the graph represents the embodied knowledge of the human experience of the absolute chronology of one's life. As humans, we cannot change the physical chronology of our lives or jump back in time. This simple fact is central to understanding the conditions faced when constructing the explicit level of a narrative. Even though physics – from relativity theory, thermodynamics, to chaos research – demonstrates that time can be undirected and reversible, we experience time as progressing within the physical reality of planet earth. Within film dramaturgy, we are convinced that everyone's individual sensual-physical experience of his/her life establishes the reference point for the construction of a narrative. These parameters regulate all variables, the point(s) of view, character design, rhythm, and the necessity of constructing a suitable chronotopos.

Dramaturgical/aesthetical linkages between situations at the beginning and the end of the story, as well as related to relevant situations throughout, give elegance to a film. This technique also supports the principle of familiarity and promotes the impression of coherence. Furthermore, such a conceptual structure of references within the cinematic narrative has a positive effect on the financial and organisational aspects of a production.

An excellent example to understand what is outlined here is Louis Malle's Au Revoir Les Enfants (Malle, F/D/I 1987). In this movie, the first scene of the fifth act mirrors the first scene of the second act. The story takes place in 1940 in a Catholic boarding school near Paris. At the beginning of the second act, a few new students arrive one night. The next day, during a history lesson, a German soldier knocks on the door. Everybody is scared. Some of the teachers fear that the German occupiers will come to search for the Jews hidden in the convent. Instead, however, the soldier asks for an opportunity to confess. Later, at the beginning of the fifth act, also during a school lesson, in the same room, another German soldier knocks on the door. This time it is not a single soldier, it's a squad, in search of Jewish students and staff.[82]

Recognition and Reverse

Anagnorisis, as the moment of recognition, and *peripeteia,* as the moment of changing the direction of the activity of the main character(s), of a reverse, are also key concepts within explicit dramaturgy. Anagnorisis and peripeteia are inseparably linked and must be arranged close together in temporal terms. Sophocles, Aristophanes, Aeschylus, and others pioneered the use of these dramatic elements in classical Greek tragedies. Aristotle drew on one particular genre of these, the myth-based tragedy, to formulate his principles of a dramatic construction in the *Poetics*. Aristotle already introduced six categories of possible forms of recognition, which allow a broad variety.[83] In most conventional screenwriting manuals, these are merged into the 'central

---

82 Cf. Stutterheim & Kaiser 2011, pp. 140–156
83 Aristoteles & Schmitt 2008, chapter 11 and 16

turning point'. This central turning point consists of these two inseparable elements, which only bring about the turn in the activity of the main character.

An anagnorisis is directed towards the main character as well as to the audience. This term defines a situation in which a motivation or obstacle affects the action of the protagonist(s). To achieve the intended impact, the protagonist can have an encounter, which leads to an understanding and changes the situation of the protagonist. The catalyst provoking this change might be a letter as in LA MALA EDUCACIÓN (Almodóvar, E 2004)[84], a newspaper article, SPELLBOUND (Hitchcock, USA 1945)[85], to get a response to a wish, THE SHINING (Kubrick, UK/USA 1980)[86], just by being confronted with the unexpected as for example when Orlando meets the queen (ORLANDO. Potter, UK/R/I/F/NL 1992), or the draughtsman whilst drawing the estate (THE DRAUGHTSMAN'S CONTRACT. Greenaway, UK 1982).

The moment of recognition must have an existential impact on the main character(s) as well as the quality and direction of the action.[87] As a result of the moment of the anagnorisis, immediately afterwards or a short time later, the condition of the main character's power to act changes and can be reversed. That means that if a character at the beginning of the story acts in response to an event, as in SPELLBOUND (Hitchcock, USA 1945), CAPE FEAR (Scorsese, USA 1992), or LA MALA EDUCACIÓN (Almodóvar, E 2004), later this character will drive the action. In SPELLBOUND, the character of the doctor understands at the moment of the anagnorisis the elements of the situation they are confronted with, and can henceforth actively shape events. In movies in which the main character has pushed the action forward until that moment, as in THE DAY OF THE JACKAL (Zinnemann, UK/F 1973) or COLLATERAL (Mann, USA 2004), an unexpected event happens at the moment of anagnorisis and hence the character has to adjust, change their approach, which manifests itself at the moment of peripeteia. Typically, a scene or sequence in the middle of the film connects both anagnorisis and peripeteia, but not always. Exceptions confirm the rule – LOST HIGHWAY (Lynch, USA 1997) is one such notable

---

84 Cf. Stutterheim & Kaiser 2011, p. 191/192
85 Cf. Stutterheim 2015, pp. 245–260
86 Cf. Ibid., pp. 49–78
87 Cf. Anderson 1962, p. 30; cf. in more detail Stutterheim 2015, pp. 136–139

exception. The representation of a decisive development is based on the dialectic of these two moments. How these two elements can be adapted and applied in modern film dramaturgy is explained in more detail in the following chapters. What needs to be emphasised here is the role and importance of these two interconnected moments in supporting logic and probability in every narrative-performative work. In films understood as "classic", anagnorisis and peripeteia are usually brought about by dialogue and action. In modern and postmodern films, these can arise from dialogue as well as from the visual narrative, supported by moments of referentiality.

A few examples from classic films may explain this definition: For SPELLBOUND, Hitchcock designs the main character, Doctor Constance Petersen (Ingrid Bergman), as a psychologist who passively reacts to events unfolding in the first half of the film. However, she discovers that the man accused of murder and identity theft, John Ballantyne (Gregory Peck), suffered a traumatic accident. Because of this trauma, he probably does not remember the situation in which the murder occurred. This is demonstrated when he reads aloud a newspaper article about the murder to the psychologist and then concludes that he must have been involved. The doctor recognises that an earlier trauma and the memory of the situation just described obviously influence each other. Now she is able to open doors of knowledge and to work towards a resolution. Consequently, from that moment on, she is portrayed as proactive and drives the action forward until the last moment when she exposes the actual murderer.[88]

In THE DAY OF THE JACKAL (Zinnemann, UK 1973) the eponymous protagonist, the 'Jackal' (Edward Fox), is introduced as an utterly confident professional, entirely in control of his world. In the moment of anagnorisis, he discovers that his secret plan to carry out an assassination had become known to the police and they are closing in on him. This information leads to the moment of peripeteia, forcing him to decide whether to give up or to continue with his plan. This moment is visualised through a road sign showing opposing directions. Evidently, in order to continue the story, the Jackal must carry out his plan. But in accordance with the dramaturgical principle of the peripeteia, the power-constellation

---

88 Cf. Stutterheim 2015, pp. 245–260; Stutterheim 2013a

changes. From this moment on the action is driven by his opponent, the detective (Michael Lonsdale). Zinnemann's film provides the blueprint for COLLATERAL (Mann, USA 2004) in which a disempowered and reactive taxi driver called Max (Jamie Foxx) is threatened by a contract killer (Tom Cruise) for the first half of the film. This imbalance of power between the characters shifts when a situation arises in which the character Max is provided with a moment of recognition. This moment, embedded in dialogue and action, occurs when Max and the killer visit Max's mother, Ida (Irma P. Hall), in hospital. Ida is critical of Max: 'He never had many friends. Always talking to himself in the mirror. It's unhealthy.'[89] Her dialogue triggers the anagnorisis and hence the peripeteia. Max has actually found someone to talk to: a lawyer who was his passenger in the very first scene of the movie. Max realises that he can stand up for himself and becomes an active player in the story. That is demonstrated in the situation in which he throws the killer's briefcase containing instructions for the next murder into the river. This moment marks the radical change which the character Max undergoes. From now on, this new version of Max increasingly determines the course of the plot. It shows how the figure frees himself from his fears and acts self-confidently, courageously and cleverly.[90]

In CAPE FEAR (Scorsese, USA 1992), writer Wesley Strick and director Scorsese demonstrate how modern dramaturgy plays with conventions. They set up a situation in which a threatened and passive character, the lawyer Sam Bowden (Nick Nolte), is given a chance to become active and steal the power from his aggressor, Max (Robert de Niro), for himself. The familiarity within this kind of situation leads us to expect a turnaround of control over the action, which however fails, instead enhancing Max's ability and pugnacity.

In NINOTCHKA (Lubitsch, USA 1939), the Russian commissar (Greta Garbo) is a character introduced as a cold personality and a cliché of a dogmatic apparatchik. After the situation in which anagnorisis and peripeteia happen, she turns into a sensual character. The character established as the antagonist to the commissar is the figure going with the name Count Leon d'Algout (Melvyn Douglas). He is portrayed as an

---

89 Mann USA 2004, min 49
90 Cf. Stutterheim 2015, pp. 161–176

aristocratic bon vivant. Lubitsch lets this character fall in love with the commissar who, at the outset, regards emotions as capitalist kitsch. In this comedy, the scene of anagnorisis and peripeteia is composed in a very distinct way. Here, Lubitsch swaps the position of anagnorisis and peripeteia. We see how the Count tries to gain the commissar's attention and sympathy. He achieves this through laughter resulting from a situation typical for a comedy – the Count struggling with the physical world.[91] For the peripeteia, Lubitsch lets the Count summarise the director's approach to think about every precious moment of life, about love, and to make someone laugh[92]. Thus, the Count asks the commissar to look at 'the whole ridiculous spectacle of life, at people being so serious, taking themselves pompously, exaggerating their own importance. If you can't think of anything else to laugh at, you can laugh at you and me. (...) Because we're an odd couple. (...) I don't want to leave you until I made you laugh, at least once.'[93] A moment later, when the Count loses his balance and falls over, Ninotchka laughs at his mishap. That breaks the ice, and she falls for him. The result of the peripeteia is emphasised by a change in the film lighting for the commisar, corresponding to her change in behaviour. Now, she becomes Ninotchka.

As these few examples demonstrate, there are several opportunities to arrange anagnorisis and peripeteia in film narrations, depending on style, form and theme of the film narration. Nevertheless, these two dramaturgical principles are fundamental, constant elements.

The End

The design of the end of a story or film is of high relevance. To design a convincing end is more challenging than it might seem at first glance. One must complete the action, at least to a certain degree. For 'classic', closed structures, the so-called 'Classic Hollywood Narrative Style', it is a must to close the action. For both forms, closed and open, a story just can't stop. One also has to create an ending that corresponds to the exposition and resolves the main

---

91 Cf. Lefèbvre, p. 48; Seesslen 1982, p. 29/30
92 Seesslen 1982, p. 69/70
93 Lubitsch USA 1939, min 43

storylines, a solution to the conflict, and the main characters have achieved their goal or at least established a situation that enables them to survive. Those who threatened the family or community are out of power or dead. A well-structured end helps the audience to detach themselves and 'cool off'.[94]

How to end a narration accordingly? In a classic narration of the closed form, it would be told that the conflict and the confrontation between the antagonistic main characters are resolved. That moment is defined as catharsis, also known as 'showdown' or denouement. In COLLATERAL (Mann, USA 2004), Max understands who the next and last victim must be. It is the lawyer who was his first guest that day. Knowing that the killer, Vincent, is on his way, Max desperately tries to call and convince the lawyer Annie that she is in danger. We see the killer making his way while she is sceptical about the warning. When Vincent smashes the door, she's not sitting at her desk and the audience can take a breath, for a moment. She is sitting in the library, still listening. The phone directory tells the killer in which office somebody is on the phone. Since the mobile phone Max uses to contact Annie runs out of power, he has to take action. Therefore, he has to find out how to use the revolver he acquired shortly before. While the killer gets closer to the lawyer, both moving carefully in the meanwhile dark library, Max finds his way up and arrives just in the nick of time. Shooting and hunting determine the showdown that stretches from the library into the city train, the MTA. Max hits Vincent. They come to sit vis-à-vis. Max says that they are 'almost at the next stop'. This sentence has an explicit meaning – to be almost at the next stop where one can call the ambulance; and an implicit meaning, Max taking control over the situation, and also, that Vincent is almost dead. Vincent repeats a question he asked already before: a man gets on the MTA here in L.A. and dies, do you think anybody notices? He dies, Max and Anna step out of the train the next station. He wraps her in his jacket, and the train continues its journey. Thus, the showdown fulfils Max' metamorphosis, swapping power around, and in the end, there is hope that this might be a happy end and, perhaps establishing a new family.

For films that follow a more open, modern dramaturgy, one can arrange the ending similarly. In EUROPA, EUROPA [Hitlerjunge Salomon] (Holland,

---

94 Schechner, p. xviii

D/F/PL 1990) for example, the pogrom of the Nazis among the Jewish population is the starting point for the action, which is comparable to a conflict. During the pogroms, the sister of the main character, Salomon (Marco Hofschneider), was killed. To protect them, Salomon and one of his older brothers, Isaak (René Hofschneider), are sent east. Mother Salomon implores both of them to stay alive no matter how and entreats the older brother to take care of them. However, shortly after, while on the run, the brothers are separated. The plot takes us through the different stages of Salomon's escape, determined by wartime events. These adventures have whirled him into a Nazi school. In the scene corresponding to catharsis, his life is again in grave danger. The war is over, and the NS regime has surrendered, the city in which Solomon finds himself is liberated by the Red Army. Wearing a Hitler Youth uniform, how can Salomon prove that he is a Jewish survivor? Serving structural balance, Solomon's older brother Isaac is now brought back into the action. He is one of the prisoners liberated from a concentration camp nearby. We are shown that Isaac immediately recognises his brother. This situation allows both characters to fulfil the task they were given at the beginning, and thus, their dramaturgical arc can be closed.

In ORLANDO, to mention one other example, in chapter eight, after a long journey through history, Orlando (Tilda Swinton) sits in a publisher's office in contemporary London. This publisher asks her for a re-write to give her novel a happy ending. She looks at us, into the camera. Then, she drives on her motorbike out of London. She and her daughter (Jessica Swinton) smile at each other. They arrive in the old castle from where the plot started. Everything is covered with white blankets. The commentary wraps the story up, connects beginning, end, and a new beginning. Orlando sits under the same tree, her daughter filming – the new poetry; and the countertenor sings from the sky to them. Potter denies a happy end, but she closes the filmic narration, opens a new level for the main character.

These examples were intended to demonstrate that the fundamental construction principles of explicit dramaturgy also serve openly narrated films.

Implicit Dramaturgy

Implicit dramaturgy covers the aesthetic aspects of a script as well as transmitting its meaning. Deriving from theatre dramaturgy, it deals with implicit, inscribed, "hidden" levels of dramaturgy relating to design and analysis. Implicit dramaturgy evokes associations and interpretations, empathy and emotions.[95] The intentional design at the implicit level involves the use of variations and elements of surprise. Its references include aspects of the zeitgeist, traditions and social reality.

These are elements of narration as well as the audio-visual design, which affect the plot. Implicit dramaturgy in a theatre context is achieved primarily through sub-text, multiple connotations, and linguistic references. In a film, implicit dramaturgy serves in addition to the issues mentioned above by using cinematic techniques, via elements of the audio-visual design. Aspects of implicit dramaturgy are for a less trained audience harder to identify than explicit ones.

> They point to dramaturgical dimensions in the overall structure of the work, which are often unrecognized, or prejudice or weight individual parts or contexts, and thus become important for the interpretation of the works. They are not merely concretizations or 'additions' of dramaturgical basic structures, which 'express' the fable, or the course of action or the conflicts in more detail. 'Implicit Dramaturgies' are special structural elements of various, often fundamental importance, although inscribed in the texts, noticeable due to their special position in the unfolding textual material. Often they are transported from the philosophical, cultural-historical, biographical and other milieus the authors' lives within, into the texts and are there to a certain extent tied up as nodes.[96]

The significance of implicit dramaturgy can be attributed to a particular 'mode of thinking' (diánonia [διάνοια]), which Aristotle describes as fundamental and Schmitt explains as follows: By following Aristotle's concept that everything has to be discussed in relation to its discipline, the 'mood of thinking' refers to rhetoric. In this sense, the mode of thinking determines everything that can be established by argument – not just by a geometric formula, but in particular when one does want to convince somebody in context of a decision revolving in action. This is the field of proving and disproving, evoking emotions, ways and means of making a decision look as convincing as possible.[97]

---

95 Cf. Rohmer 2000
96 Ibid., p. 15
97 Schmitt 2008b, p. 581/582

Aristotle's approach can support the author/director in developing a story that is believable and convincing. This quality evolves best from an apparent attitude of the author/director and is directed towards the audience. 'All in all, the creative act is not performed by the artist alone; the spectator brings the work in contact with the external world by deciphering and interpreting its inner qualifications and thus adds his contribution to the creative act.'[98] A writer/director, as well as every dramaturg, is always aware of the nature of art as a communicative act.

This 'mode of thinking' helps the author/director to develop a story, which is believable and convincing – in the sense that it fits the general perception of what might be true and necessary. An author/director having a clear vision for their project will most successfully achieve this quality. Implicit dramaturgy is anchored in the characters and their dialogue but also through the set and colour design and/or sound design and music. It stretches to include every aesthetic aspect of the film. In addition to the basic story, the audience – utilising their general knowledge, special interests or even their knowledge about theatre – are provided with impulses that stimulate their imagination and draws them deeper into the story. Or, if the film is postmodern, it will increase the audience's enjoyment by reflecting on the film's meaning.[99] Implicit dramaturgy unfolds through interaction with explicit dramaturgy. Thus, even when dealing with more abstract and demanding subjects, the author/director and her team can evoke a vivid and emotional effect and conversely, mainstream blockbusters or films which appear to be pure entertainment, can deal with a sophisticated subject matter. THE DAY AFTER TOMORROW (Emmerich, USA 2004), INSIDE MAN (S. Lee, USA 2006), SHUTTER ISLAND (Scorsese, USA 2010) and THE FIFTH ELEMENT (Besson, F 1997) are good examples.

Explicit and Implicit in Interaction – THE FIFTH ELEMENT

One of the best examples of a broad audience postmodern film, which demonstrates the interconnection of explicit and implicit dramaturgy, is THE FIFTH ELEMENT, written and directed by Luc Besson. The core of

---

98 Duchamp 2007 (1957), 7:01 min
99 Cf. Stutterheim 2013d

the implicit level in the film is the legend of the Holy Grail as described by Wolfram von Eschenbach in *Parzival*.[100] Eschenbach's main characters, Gaiwan and Parzival, are physically and mentally strong knights. Only together can they find the Holy Grail and consequently heal the suffering of the land. Since the early Middle Ages, the Grail legend has been associated with the Cathar, a sect that founded a church against Roman Catholicism. The Cathari were also known as *"perfecti"* or "Good People".[101] The latter is an essential aspect of the analysis of THE FIFTH ELEMENT as follows. Over the course of twenty years, the Albigensian Crusade and Inquisition crushed the Cathar in 1229. The defeat was inscribed in the peace contract of Meaux and included the appropriation of the Languedoc by France.[102] The many extraordinarily cruel events of this period are well-remembered in France; and form part of the country's cultural memory.

THE FIFTH ELEMENT weaves these familiar structural and cultural elements into a new variant of the well-known legend of the Holy Grail and the historical events it is based on, thus creating an entertaining and captivating film. Knowledge of the implicit historical-cultural references is not required to enjoy the movie. The audience, which knows neither the *Parsifal*-legend nor the history of the Cathar, will still feel entertained. Precisely designed conceptual and implicit levels of dramaturgy guarantee a convincing and entertaining effect since all elements work together. And a film should not be perceived as a riddle but unfold its power implicitly.

Luc Besson composes his film as a five-act structure. He enriches this pattern with elements of the structure of legends such as the Grail Legend, creating proximity to the model of the 'hero's journey'.[103] Given the topic, it seems apposite for Besson to use myth as the structural basis for his science-fiction adventure.

The first scene of the film, corresponding to a prelude, is set in a temple in Egypt shortly before the outbreak of the First World War. This scene is filmed in a way that plays with genre conventions and audience expectations. It is also full of implicit references, which broaden the context, initiate

---

100 Eschenbach 1994
101 Arnold 2001, p. 139
102 Ibid., p. 3; Daxelmüller, 1996, p. 144
103 Vogler 2007

the theme and make for great comedy. Focusing on the implicit drama-turgy, the story evolves as follows: In the first scene, an archaeologist (John Bluthal) is about to uncover and "translate" an old inscription that shows how the world can be saved from ultimate evil: 'When the three planets are in eclipse, the black hole, like a door, is open. Evil comes, spreading terror and chaos. See the snake, Billy? The ultimate evil.'[104] The archaeologist's assistant, Billy (Luke Perry), asks how often this is supposed to occur and the archaeologist replies, 'every 5,000 years'. This situation introduces the theme of the film; the world is endangered, threatened by an evil power, but there is still hope of redemption. 'You see here these different people or symbols of people, gathering together the four elements of life. Water, fire, earth, air. Around the fifth one, the fifth element.'[105] In the French Tarot, the fifth card is the High Priest, and the highest priests amongst the Cathar were female.

For an understanding of the use of implicit dramaturgy, it should also be noted that Egypt is an important pilgrimage site as well as a place of imag-ination for traditional and alternative "believers". It is the region where many of the stories of the *Torah/Old Testament* take place, often telling of the struggle of good against evil, of the struggle for survival. Besides, it was assumed that crucial knowledge required to keep the world safe was stored in the hidden chambers of pyramids.[106]

The inscription deciphered by the archaeologist is "hidden knowledge", guarded by a Franciscan monk who soon arrives at the temple. The fact that the monk intends to poison the archaeologist underscores the gravity of the discovery. His plan fails due to an amusing cultural misunderstanding which signals the postmodern convention of using comic irony as style.[107] The archaeologist explains the plot in another piece of dialogue: 'It is like a battle plan. Here the good, here the evil. And here a weapon against evil.'[108]

Just in time, the Knights of the Holy Grail – the Mondoshawan – ar-rive to rescue the secret weapon. A looming war poses an even more

---

104 Besson, F 1997, min 3
105 Ibid., min 4
106 Blavatsky 1960
107 Cf. Despoix 2003, pp. 236–244; Stutterheim 2013d
108 Besson, F 1997, min 4

significant threat to it than the archaeologist. The knights whisk it away to safety somewhere far away from earth, promising to return it when needed.

The next sequence introduces that dangerous moment, three hundred years on: evil in the form of a fiery comet is threatening to destroy the earth. Every earthly weapon the US Army is going to send against this deadly comet simply enriches the comet's power. In desperation, the Mondoshawan sent a space ship to bring the secret weapon back to earth. Establishing the conflict on two levels – one abstract and general, the other concrete and immediate and acted out by characters connected to the evil comet – Besson introduces the antagonist: a Goebbels-Hitler-pastiche (Gary Oldman). The antagonist's soldiers destroy the Mondoshawan spaceship. Only the hand of one of the pilots survives, and it is used to reconstruct Leeloo (Milla Jovovitch). This very human looking Mondoshawan represents the principle of Parsifal. Like Parsifal, Leeloo, who grew up far from the human world, speaks no English and has to learn it. Her character is established as the spiritual power, the only one capable of activating the secret weapon to defeat evil. Analogous to the Parsifal poem, Besson couples her with the earthly knight, an experienced and brave ex-major called Korban Dallas (Bruce Willis). He represents Gawain. Only by working together can they solve the problem and save the world.

The scene that introduces Korban Dallas combines explicit, direct action with the implicit dramaturgy of the Parsifal-Cathar-reference. When asked about his status as a single man, the ex-major replies that he is still waiting to meet the 'perfect woman'. This is going to happen soon afterwards. Besson concentrates his explicit narration on their evolving relationship. Obviously they both have to return to the temple, the place where the film began, in order to trigger the secret weapon. Leeloo turns out to be the fifth element, the 'perfect man', as a version of the 'perfecti'. Many more examples could be teased out to explain the implicit dramaturgy in THE FIFTH ELEMENT, but hopefully, this one example demonstrates its application. Other films with similar well designed implicit levels are THE SHINING (Kubrick, UK/USA 1980), STALKER (Tarkovsky, USSR 1979), SHUTTER ISLAND (Scorsese, USA 2010) and BLACK SWAN (Aronofski, USA 2010) to name but a few.

Brief Summary Film Dramaturgy

Dramaturgy applies to all elements of the aesthetic composition of audio-visual and narrative-performative time-based works, of which films are part. A film is produced as an entertaining and captivating work of art to be screened to an audience. With the performance, the aim of the production is fulfilled. Therefore, all aspects of the production have to merge into one consistent work. They can't and should not be separated - not in the production phase neither in the analysis, from a dramaturgical point of view. Accordingly, the Dramaturgy is dedicated to the entire work that is going to be performed, not just to the text it is developed from. Dramaturgy as practice promotes and supports the creative process throughout the development of the work. Ideally, from the very first idea to the day of the premiere, and if possible in an advisory capacity for events around the release of the film. Dramaturgical knowledge forms the conceptual basis for the organisation of structure, designing of the sujet, development of the story, as well as corresponding character design and the design of the audio-visual narrative. It gives a backbone to every production.

Dramaturgy can also serve as an analytical method or support an analysis of a film as well as any other narrative-performative artwork. Dramaturgical knowledge enables the researcher to recognise aesthetic means and artistic approaches that help to give an artwork or film its particular effect, as well as the ability to identify where a film fails to captivate its audience. Aesthetic analysis and philosophical reflection in dramaturgy are inseparable. Both are philosophical sub-disciplines. Dramaturgical knowledge and examination enable interpretations in which creative and artistic decisions can be taken into account and in which it is understood what influence they have on the overall effect, but also to recognise the limitations of designs. Dramaturgical knowledge enables a better understanding of the immanent processes inscribed in a work that has a particular impact on the audience. They are always connected with cultural, moral, religious and social traditions, regional peculiarities and the zeitgeist.

'The Big Five' – Basic Dramaturgic Rules

The five fundamental dramaturgical rules presented below are of equal importance. They derive from collating traditions, academic knowledge, and professional experiences in film productions, thus respecting a wide range of publications[109] and responses on the topic.

When adopting dramaturgical knowledge and practices for film and media productions one must always reflect on specifics of the media, in particular, technological and production circumstances. Differences between time-based audio-visual media and theatre or live performance influence the aesthetics and, hence, one must respect these in the dramaturgical approach. The most obvious in this regard is the physical appearance of the actor, who in theatre or live performances enters and leaves a stage or other places of action in person. Their movement can't be shortened or cut away. In a film, it is not common or necessary to show every movement of a figure, and hence movements from one place to another can be cut short.

Non-Replaceable and Immovable

Following the re-publishing, translations, and interpretations of Aristotle's *Poetics*,[110] writers and directors have been aware of the general principle that every element, every word and every gesture, as well as all masks, signs, colour choices and production details in a dramatic performative work, have to be determined as irreplaceable and unmovable. One should compose an action in such a way that not a single one of its parts could be taken out or moved without harming or changing the narrative. What may or may not be there without discernible difference is not a constituting part of the whole.[111] Arthur Miller, for example, admired Henrik Ibsen because 'nothing in his plays exists for itself, not a smart line, not a gesture that can be isolated. It was breath-taking.'[112] In a dramatic narrative, one has to overcome the chaos of events as they appear in real life.[113] A dramatic action should be developed organically out of a lively centre as well as a clear thematic and aesthetic approach to be found in every aspect of the work.

If a situation, a gesture, a word or dialogue, a shot or sequence can be removed or changed without affecting the situation or the action, then this

---

109 Cf. Blothner 1999; Carrière 2003; Mamet 1991a; Murch 2001; Pearlman 2009
110 Aristoteles & Schmitt 2008
111 Ibid., 2008, chapter 8, a30–a35
112 Miller, 1958, p. 180
113 Cf. Carrière & Bonitzer 1999, pp. 178–185

element is unnecessary. Such an element interrupts the immersive experience because it causes loss of attention.

In the Moment

Observing an event or action in everyday life is always perceived at the very moment and in the present. A film addresses most of our senses at the same time, corresponding to our physical experience of the story-world. Some film productions present an illusion of reality, while other directors try to relativise or break this. Notwithstanding how fantastic the events on screen may be, through the aesthetic attraction the audience witnesses the events unfolding. This is why the audience has an emotional response to a film, even though it is aware of the unreality of the occurence.[114] Accordingly, one would like to develop a film narrative that captivates the viewer throughout. "If it interests me so much that I forget the rest of the world, I live two hours in that story, tied up and taken prisoner by it. And I want to know the end."[115]

The creation of a moment that originates an "illusion of reality" within the narrated cosmos of a film requires a conscious approach to the organisation of information. Everything that contributes to the understanding of the unfolding action must be introduced in a particular order. In the composition of the dramaturgy of a cinematic plot, it is therefore essential to always be aware of the situation in which the audience experiences the progress of the plot as being in the present. Relevant information can be provided by image and sound, set design or *gestus*, explicit or implicit. What the audience needs to know, see or hear to understand the chain of events must, therefore, be organised accordingly.

Probability

The physical world which we live in and experience as our reality can be represented in a realistic or naturalistic style, artistically transformed, abstracted or turned into a metaphor. Regardless, the events depicted must appear as plausible as possible. Employing the logic of the film, every

---

114 Lotman 1977, p. 21
115 Carrière 1999, p. 143

character, situation, and development should be credible and convincing. This principle of probability evolved from the history of the performing arts, in particular through a tradition known as the Mimesis-Principle, one of the constant elements of dramatic narration.[116] Already Aristotle demanded probability for the narration of a tragedy in the *Poetics*.[117] This principle has been discussed and developed further by many authors and directors over time. It is not just applicable for narrating an action but also valid for designing characters. Authors create characters derived from their perception of the world. Even in realism, the *Mimesis*-Principle is understood as an artistic discovery of the world, as interpretation through representation.[118] Illusion, deriving from artistic reflection of experienced reality, can be representative and imaginative at the same time. Thus, a 'second truth' emerges, which is often more focused than the one we might happen to experience in real life. Carrière writes that real life is never as exciting and structured as a movie although it might appear attractive at the moment.[119]

Achieving quality of plausibility also enables continuity. Thus, every character, every sentence, every situation and every detail corresponds to the rules defined within the exposition and by the chronotopos as planted for this particular story. In modern dramaturgy, the overall theme, which gives every single segment its significance and focuses the action, is defined as *Bedeutungsfazit*[120], the "essential meaning".[121] This is embedded in implicit dramaturgy, it can also be apparent to the audience as part of explicit dramaturgy.

To Surprise within the Familiar

With each film, one wants to tell a new and fascinating story or a familiar one in a new way. Each new plot and each interpretation embodies an

---

116 Metschler 2010, Girshausen, 2005
117 Aristoteles & Schmitt 2008, chapter 7, a10–a15
118 Metschler 2010, p. 646/647
119 Carrière 1999, p. 133
120 cf. Klotz 1980, p. 112; Stutterheim 2015, pp. 216–219
121 Ibid

adventure in itself. Based on the relationship between the storyteller and their audience, one can classify three different forms of familiarity:

– Someone tells an audience a story, which is new to them. The challenge here is to win the audience over to something new and unknown. By using familiar patterns in the construction of the opening scene and implicit dramaturgy, a viewer can be invited into an unfamiliar new world.

– Someone tells a story to an audience that is also familiar with the plot. These may be either historical narratives or adaptations of well-known literature. Characters, turning points, and the ending are generally known. The interest arises from the new interpretation of heroes and events.[122] A familiar story is enriched by its retelling. The writer/director conveys a new approach and invites the audience to experience the story anew. "When we tell a familiar story to people who know about it, we try to introduce a new, unknown element that more or less changes perspective; otherwise boredom threatens to overtake storytellers and listeners alike."[123]

– Somebody improvises an unknown story to an audience that is also unfamiliar with it. This leads to further improvisation and usually takes place in live performances.

No matter which of these three versions of telling a story applies, with the dramaturgical approach one can establish a balance between the known and unknown to attract an audience.

Show, Don't Tell

Unlike its televisual cousin, historically, film, drama as well as documentaries, were narrative-performative art. In film, the spoken dialogue was secondary. Especially in modern and postmodern films, image and sound contribute significantly to the development of the plot and are more than elements of a mise-en-scène. In such films, a cinematic or aesthetic conflict[124] may replace or support a dramatic conflict.

---

122 Carrière & Bonitzer 1999, p. 133
123 Ibid., p. 92/93
124 Eisenstein 2001; cf. Stutterheim 2015, pp. 134–135

The dramatic conflict in the classic and closed form of a narrative is the event that sets into action the antagonistic constellation that arose at the beginning of the film. In such a plot constellation, the central figure and its opponent lead the action.

The concept of a cinematic or aesthetic conflict derives from Eisenstein's definition of the 'Visual Counterpoint'.[125] Such a visual counterpoint makes it possible to present certain principles of a film's "grammar" that are not bound by but related to the spoken word. The visual conflict applies in particular to the syntax of film-aesthetic expression. The shot and its image composition are not only technical elements but part of the narrative.[126] The cinematic conflict results from the aesthetic composition. To achieve this requires the establishment of a dialectical concept as a foundation to the visual conflict, a conflict demonstrated in the details in every frame that comes into effect through a particular montage of the shots. Resulting from the concept of the visual counterpoint, Eisenstein lists ten different types of conflict constellations: graphic conflict, conflict of light, conflict of space, of volumes, of tempo, or conflict resulting from optical or special distortion. Another form of this concept is the visual-tonal conflict resulting in film syntax. This cinematic or aesthetic conflict represents a further stage of the visual conflict, now combining not just the image detail but also the sound design in the composition described above.[127]

In this sense, even places that are far apart can be related to each other in an image, as in SHUTTER ISLAND (Scorsese, USA 2010). This is complemented by the visualisation of emotional states or imagination.

The design of visual and acoustic levels is of vital importance within dramaturgy. Audio-visual design, as part of implicit dramaturgy, can contribute to the meaningful expression of the action. Image and sound design can support both to surprise within the familiar and provide the familiar in the unfamiliar. A deliberate dramaturgical approach gives consistency to a story, helps to establish a reference to reality, and as a result serving the aspect of probability.

---

125 Eisenstein (1951) 2001
126 Ibid.
127 Cf. Eisenstein 2006

Fig. 15: An Example for a Cinematic Conflict

This first chapter gave an overview about the principles and traditions of dramaturgy, and also presented a very condensed summary of earlier publications written and published in German.[128] It is intended as a foundation for the following introduction of the diverse opportunities given within modern dramaturgy.

---

128 Frejlich 1964; Hasche, Kalisch, & Weber 2014; Stutterheim 2015; Stutterheim & Kaiser 2011

Essential Dramaturgical Features of Modern Films

The following section of the book presents selected and relevant principles of modern dramaturgy, serving films that are often described as poetic or cinematic and sometimes also as postmodern. Other authors call these forms 'alternative', 'breaking the rules'[129], or as of 'stylish style'.[130] The dramaturgical patterns of traditions of narrative-performative art, in short: drama, are applied to these movies classified as poetic or creative, or 'non-Aristotelian'.

These dramaturgical models emerged from three categories of drama, which Aristotle only referred to in his *Poetics*,[131] but did not discuss. Essential aspects of dramaturgical knowledge supporting movies to be classified as open[132] or modern, including all terms mentioned above are introduced throughout the following chapters.

'Non-Aristotelian' Narration

In Ancient Western Theatre alternative forms of drama already existed, which are neither conflict based, nor hero-driven or narrated in a linear causal structure. These forms of drama were not of secondary importance, but Aristotle was simply not interested in them. It should be briefly pointed out here that Aristotle was a philosopher, and his main interests were science, nature, logic and rhetoric.[133] These categories of dramatic performative art are less hero-driven. One of these is dedicated to present moments of misery and pathos, therefore called 'pathos tragedy'. Characteristic of this form is that the protagonist reflects with fervour and emotion on their state resulting from an event, idea, or situation. The second category contains plays in which the characters express characteristics of human

---

129 Cf. Dancyger & Rush 2013
130 Cf. Bordwell 2006, p. 115 et sequ.
131 Aristoteles & Schmitt 2008
132 Klotz 1980
133 Guthrie & Warren, 2013, pp. 113–131

behaviour and ethos. The third category of drama emphasises the moment of thinking, diánoia. This particular understanding of thinking/reflection is demonstrated through dialogue, character traits, and appropriate action expressing all these aspects.[134]

It is worth mentioning here that the open, non-linear narrative is neither new nor unfamiliar; it was used as far back as the *Torah*. The Old Testament is chronologically arranged, while the Torah is organised according to liturgical importance. Therefore, it is non-linear, non-causal, and textured.[135] Gertrud Stein (1874–1946)[136] reflects, in her particularly modern style of writing, on that concept in one of her lectures on *Narration*:[137]

> In a kind of a way what has made the Old Testament such permanently good reading is that really in a way in the Old Testament writing there really was not any such thing there was not really any succession of anything and really in the Old Testament there is really no sentence existing and no paragraphing, think about this thing, think if you have not really been knowing this thing and then let us go on telling about what paragraphs and sentences have been what prose and poetry has been. So then in the Old Testament writing there is really no actual conclusion that anything is progressing that one thing is succeeding another thing, that anything in that sense in the sense of succeeding happening is a narrative of anything, but most writing is based on this thing most writing has been a real narrative writing a telling of the story of anything in the way that thing has been happening and now everything is not that thing there is a present not a sense of anything being successively happening, moving is in every direction beginning and ending can know anything at any time that anything is happening and so really and truly is there any sentence and any paragraphing is there prose and poetry as the same thing or different things is there now any narrative of any successive thing.[138]

The *Torah/Old Testament* tells individual stories, which are representative for a group of people, for a historical event or change. Thus they are

---

134 Aristoteles & Schmitt 2008, p. 25

135 Cf. Liss, Boeckler, and Landthaler 2011, p. 1; Koschorke 2012, p. 57/58

136 Gertrud Stein was an American novelist, poet, playwright, and art collector. She became famous as a center figure of the impressionism and avant-garde art movement in Paris. Stein is most remembered for her novels *The Making of Americans* (1906–08; 1925), *The Autobiography of Alice B. Toklas* (1933) and *Gertrude Stein, Everybody's Autobiography* (1937)

137 Eco 1990 (1977), p. 31 et seq., p. 154

138 Stein 1935, p. 19

connected with a collective experience. This principle is central for the modern and open dramaturgy as well.

In the modern world, the drama is no longer absolute. In a drama, which is of absolute character, its structural character of homogeneity creates an illusion of showing an entity independent of historical events.

> Because the Drama is always primary, its internal time is always the present. That in no way means that the Drama is static, only that the time passes in a particular manner: the present passes and becomes the past and, as such, can no longer be present on stage. As the present passes away, it produces change, a new present springs from its antithesis. In the Drama, time unfolds as an absolute, linear sequence in the present. Because the Drama is absolute, it is itself responsible for this temporal sequence. It generates its own time.[139]

By changing the structure and adding a level of narration independent of the interpersonal dialogue, the illusion of mirroring reality will be dismantled. The dramatic action is replaced by a scenic narration and the appropriate modern dramaturgy[140], which will be outlined in more detail below.

Throughout theatre history in Europe, 'non-aristotelian' forms of drama evolved and were developed by authors such as William Shakespeare (1564–1616 or 1550–1604),[141] Jean Racine (1639–1699), Molière (Jean-Baptiste Poquelin, 1622–1673), Karoline von Günderode (1780–1808), Georg Büchner (1813–37), Antonin Artaud (1896–1906), Bertolt Brecht (1898–1956), and Heiner Müller (1929–95) or Yasmina Reza (1959-), to mention just a few. Dramatic writing resulting from a tradition these authors represent is often described as 'open form' or Modern Drama.[142] The differentiation between dramaturgy of a closed and an open form relates to the structure of explicit dramaturgy. As mentioned already, a closed dramatic narrative presents the action as absolute,[143] and is represented through a pattern sometimes referred to as the 'Hollywood Formula'. As an audience, we follow a story unfolding before our eyes and – when well made – it casts a spell over us, regardless of whether it follows an open

---

139 Szondi 1987, p. 9
140 Ibid., p. 84
141 Kreiler 2009
142 Szondi 1965, 1987
143 Szondi 1965, p. 140; 1987, p. 85

or closed dramaturgy. In a movie using a closed form of dramaturgy, the conflict will be resolved, and the action completed at the end of the movie. No substantial questions will be left unanswered, the hero will survive, the family will have been rescued or the hero will have found love enabling him to establish his own family.

Open form drama patterns have been part of film dramaturgy throughout screenwriting history, even in Hollywood studio productions. Although manuals published in the last few decades may give the impression of a 'classic' form, a close look at films made in Hollywood or the USA since the beginning of film production reveals that there is no dominant form to representing such imaginary narrative.[144] The term 'classic Hollywood style', refers to a particular period and summarises a mix of works of open and closed forms under this umbrella terminology. Altogether, most of the different and also distinct influences which are referred to in the course of this book are summarised by Bordwell as classic, who writes that 'all reappear in Hollywood dramaturgy, and all are defined in cause and effect.'[145] A few titles should be mentioned here to give an impression of the diverse range of dramaturgical traditions used in Hollywood productions: THE TEN COMMANDMENTS (DeMille USA 1923), GREED (Stroheim, USA 1924), GONE WITH THE WIND (Fleming, USA 1939), CITIZEN KANE (Welles, USA 1941), BEN HUR (Wyler, USA 1959), 2001 – A SPACE ODYSSEY (Kubrick, UK/USA 1968), THE USUAL SUSPECTS (SINGER, USA/G 1995), and many more movies made by Ida Lupino, Dorothy Arzner, John Carpenter, Quentin Tarantino, Martin Scorsese, Stanley Kubrick, Darren Aronofsky, and others.

The concept of the open form allows the most considerable possible detachment from the structure of the linear causal organisation. The concept of a style of modern movies also enables us to free ourselves from a naturalistic understanding of the representation of reality.[146] The modern filmmaker allows an open relationship of non-uniqueness amongst the work, themselves as the artist/director/filmmaker, and the audience. Thus, members of the audience are invited to establish their particular relationship

144 cf. Maras 2009; Staiger 1996; Thompson 1999
145 Bordwell, Staiger, & Thompson 2006, p. 9
146 Ibid.,

to the work.[147] If a film corresponds to the open form, then the audience is invited to follow the action as an active participant. One is asked to think along and interpret the story as it develops.

Modern and Poetic — Open Dramaturgy

The fundamentals of poetic, modern and postmodern films are shaped by the use of dramatic and dramaturgical rules evolving from Modern Drama. Volker Klotz, Umberto Eco, Peter Weiss, and Peter Szondi analysed and described rules for the modern drama from which modern film dramaturgy derives.[148]

When opting for a modern, poetic, open form, the writer/director can combine patterns from established drama traditions, film genre conventions, art history, performative, and experimental art. Brecht, Piscator, and Reinhardt experimented with open dramaturgy in the 1920s. Their achievements provided the basis for modern film dramaturgy as outlined previously. Deriving from this tradition, one can define the opportunities to arrange an open structured work. To put it succinctly, modern film dramaturgy offers patterns and models to organise a work resulting in an open relationship between the work and the audience, allowing association and interpretation.[149]

The general dramaturgical structure gives open dramaturgy its stable ground, as well as supporting the effect of familiarity. Everything introduced here derives from the tradition of dramaturgy.[150]

Epic Theatre – Poetic cinema

The Modern film, alternatively labelled as Poetic Cinema, originated in the 1920s. It is a relative of epic theatre, and they evolved in correspondence, in a dialogue with each other. Thus, modern dramaturgy is the heart of the modern film, also known as poetic cinema. Arthur Miller,

---

147 Bordwell et al., 2006, p. 17
148 Klotz 1980; Eco 1989; Weiss 1995; Szondi 1965, 1987
149 Cf. Eco 1989, Szondi 1987, Klotz 1980, Stutterheim 2015, pp. 197–200, Balázs 2001, p. 85 et seq.
150 Cf. in more detail in chapter one and in Balázs 2001, p. 85

Tennessee Williams, Bertolt Brecht, Erwin Piscator, Max Reinhardt, Erich von Stroheim, and Béla Balázs, were all influential agents in this regard. Since then these were joined by Maya Deren, Peter Brook, Jean-Claude Carrière, and Ariane Mnouchkine, Jim Jarmusch, Sally Potter, Deepa Meetha, to mention just a few.

Modern dramaturgy inherits a dialectic worldview.[151] The modern, epic drama aims to transform a condition into a process. Since historical situations and social circumstances are human-made, they can be challenged and changed by us. Brecht believed that a director must carve out the materialist process. Too much emotional identification obstructs critical reflection. The realistic narration would show that the character changes under the influence of the events – by doing so, empathic identification is no longer possible. Epic theatre is sensual and poetic but in the sense of materialist philosophy.[152] Its aesthetic includes all possible forms of expression and communication – from set design, costume, masks, to music and poetry.[153] Epic theatre is *gestisch* which can be translated as referential.[154] A gestus demonstrates the social significance and application of dialectics.[155]

Epic theatre or narrative-performative art has a long tradition within the theatre tradition worldwide. In this context, the term epic refers to a specific aesthetic of the theatrical performance. Therefore, music, dance, emblematic gestus, symbolic and metaphoric techniques are employed. For example, in the *No-Theatre* tradition, actors introduce their character when entering the stag: 'I am character x.' In a *Kabuki*-performance, a narrator or stage manager welcomes the audience and presents a summary of the plot. Traditional Chinese theatre also is epic and episodic, often including erratic or surprising turns and developments. Movements in time and space are symbolised.[156] The Common Players, who performed at the end of the 16th and early 17th century in England, belong within the epic tradition. The performers interacted with the audience, and the characters introduced

---

151 In more detail in Stutterheim, 2015; Stutterheim & Kaiser, 2011
152 Cf.Brecht, 1966a, 1966d, 1966e, 1966f
153 Stein & Wilder 2010
154 Benjamin 1977, p. 521
155 Ibid., p. 530
156 Fiebach 2015, p. 71–74

themselves. They performed in the courtyards of pubs on a simple plat-form.[157] These features of addressing the audience, emphasising the artifi-ciality, highlighting the acting as the act of interpretation or impersonation of a character, are equally quintessential for epic movies.

Considering storytelling in regard to screenwriting, Jean-Claude Carrière argued that one could, in general, categorise stories into two types: one is the in the Western world dominant type of linear and caus-ally structured movies. Stories of this category tell about events which happen in a specific time frame. These are classified as closed forms, which are predominantly referred to as classic. The other type of storytelling is "oriental, serpentine, and endless".[158] This type of story is continually renewing itself all the time.[159] Epic stories are found all over the world, for example, the *Mahābhārata*[160], *Genji Monogatari*[161], *One Thousand and One Nights*[162], *Don Quixote*[163], *The Tale of Genji*[164], *Münchhausen*[165], *The Good Soldier Švejk*[166], and many more. All of these are examples of a slowly progressing narrative. Carrière describes these stories as follows: a main character begins a journey to travel to new places, then decides to take a break, sit for a moment in the shadow of a tree, eat a bite and drink a sip of wine before continuing their journey. Unexpectedly, this first character is joined by someone else who is thirsty or has just survived an adventure. They begin to talk, and hence, into the main story of the long walk into an unknown region, with which the story began, a completely different and new story is woven in.[167] This description of epic narration also recalls the narrative technique used by Geoffrey Chaucer in *The Canterbury Tales*, written in the late 14th century.[168] This epic story tells

---

157 Fiebach 2015, p. 122/123
158 Bonitzer & Carrière 1999, p. 204
159 Szondi 1987, p. 5/6
160 Brecht 1966b, 1966f
161 Bonitzer & Carrière 1999, p. 203/204
162 Smith 2009
163 Cervantes Saavedra 1810
164 Murasaki & Tyler, 2001
165 Burton, Finamore, & Lopez 1985
166 Hašek 1973
167 Bonitzer & Carrière 1999, p. 206
168 Bürger & Raspe 1968

of a pilgrimage. The narrator accidentally meets other pilgrims in a tavern at the gates of London, and then these travel together to Canterbury. Along the way, the pilgrims tell each other their stories. The narrator is a prototype of the central self that is part of the group. Other European examples from the history of literature and theatre could be cited here, e.g. Joseph Conrad (1857–1924), Anna Seghers (1900–1983), and Christa Wolf (1921–2011), but this would digress from our discussion of film dramaturgy. However, it is important to mention this in order to show that the tradition of telling stories is more varied than some people assume or represent today. In the age of industrialisation, epic storytelling has probably been displaced by a more hierarchical way of storytelling, focussed towards a specific goal to be achieved.

An epic narrative can begin when a character feels the urge or is forced to embark on a search, a change and a journey. The trigger can be curiosity, an inconspicuous impulse or external factors. The journey itself can be a real one in the physical world, or an inner search or even spiritual odyssey. The referential [*gestisch*] style of an epic narration, its visual and sensual presentation of an artistic-poetic transformation of materialist processes, invites the audience to observe and relate. Therefore, epic narratives follow particular aesthetic parameters: Portrayed is that the situation of the characters is influenced by circumstances that elude their influence. That this is the case is not only illustrated. In the course of the action, this situation is depicted and emphasized. In contemplating this action, the audience can relate to it. An essential feature of an epic narration is to show dissonances as they might happen as well in real life, and how these can influence other characters who are more or less involved in the event. A precise observation is as central to epic movies as it is a feature of epic theatre. The audience is invited by this artistic practice to think along, to compare.[169] With the help of irony, one can emphasise a situation and at the same time assist the audience distancing from the witnessed events. The irony is a significant feature of the epic theatre, as well as of modern and post-modern film.

---

169 Cf. Fiebach 2015, pp. 269–273; Brecht 1977, 1964

Explicit Dramaturgy and Scenic Structure for Modern Film

The following section introduces essential features of modern dramaturgy. These principles either serve as supplements or are a variant to the dramaturgical basis demonstrated above.

Core features of modern film dramaturgy are:

- All elements of the movie reflect on the [Bedeutungsfazit] 'essential meaning' as defined earlier, which encapsulates the theme the film represents. In films which are designed as modern or open, a theme also can replace the conflict. There may also be potential for conflict resulting from such trope that does not have to be expressed in direct physical action but might be presented as either dialectical conflict, moral conflict, or judgement conflict.
- A backstory is not needed any longer (but possible).
- The narration can be arranged in a fragmented and non-linear structure; narrative threads can be parallel or inverted.
- A dramatic conflict in the sense of the hero-driven tragedy is no longer needed, but an incident or event triggering the action is required to echo the concept of the conflict.
- One central hero is no longer required, nor are heroic actions. It is possible to arrange one or several protagonists to lead the plot. Consequently, it is possible to understand two persons acting together, next to each other or far apart, in a way which can be recognised as one dramaturgical central character. The design of characters follows according to different principles.
- The film narrative has to be composed in a way that the narration comes to an end; although not all questions need to be answered nor all problems resolved: in a modern film, one does not have to provide a definitive solution (but you do need an ending!).

Scenic Narration

In modern dramaturgy, the linear causal construction of traditional drama is transformed into a scenic narration. Volker Klotz describes the open dramatic form as "the whole in sections".[170] The overall theme, the intention of the author represented through the 'essential meaning [Bedeutungsfazit], holds all the segments together. It corresponds with the interest and world-view of the author/director and is their motivation for telling this particular story. The theme and the dramatic idea behind what is presented can be of a more significant concept than the concrete action at the explicit level is conveyed at first sight. In modern films, the individual sections of the plot no longer strictly emerge out of the previous ones but are arranged accordingl to such a thematic concept. Hence, the story can be composed as fragments and not chronologically. The events unfold independently from the activities of the main character(s) but influence their situation and consequently cause action. The mise-en-scène becomes metaphoric. The illusion of reality no longer has to be evoked, but can be deployed for specific reasons. The elements of the plot can be fragmentary and connected through associations. With the help of explicit and implicit dramaturgy, one can create a metaphoric narrative. Sensual and aesthetic means are just as crucial for this form of composition as the handling of constants and variants.

A complex story that unfolds through a metaphor can be as moving as a conventionally narrated drama, especially since one might present it on the level of the explicit dramaturgy in accordance with classic drama. To be able to tell a metaphoric story, one should consider a dramaturgical concept from the outset. Here, too, the basic rules introduced above must be taken into account. The principles outlined previously are the blueprint for film dramaturgy. In the open form, flexibility results from the consideration of the essential elements of dramaturgy. The graph below is designed to provide an understanding of the relationship of possible flexibility to the fundamental structure that is still the backbone. All of this is an integral part of the scenic narrative and will be explained in more detail below.

---

170 Klotz 1980, p. 115

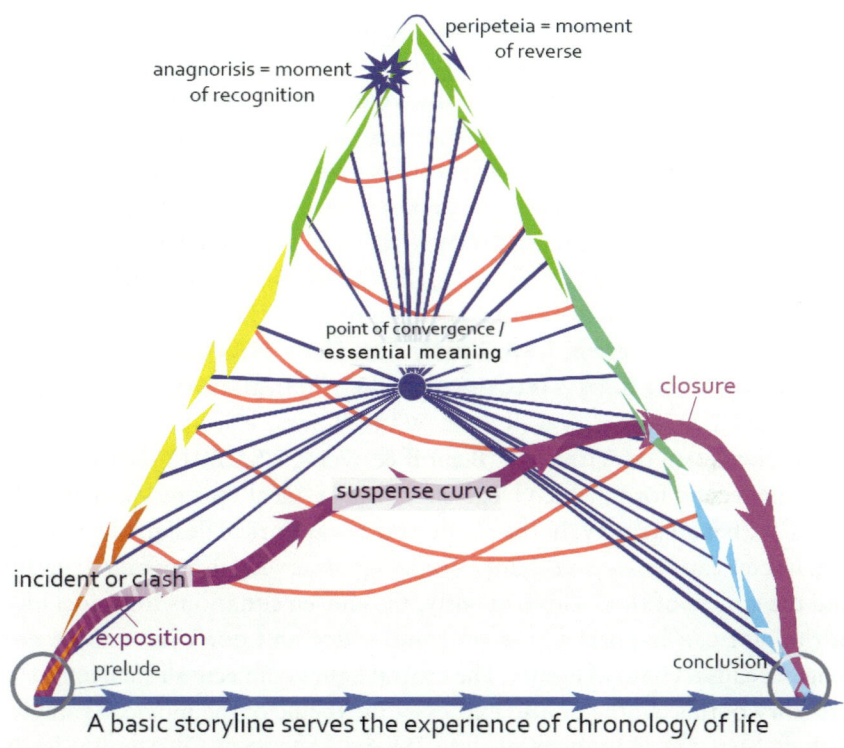

A basic storyline serves the experience of chronology of life

(c) Kerstin Stutterheim & Jasper Stutterheim

Fig. 16: Construction Scheme for the Open Form Dramaturgy. © Kerstin Stutterheim & Jasper Stutterheim

Ideal Starting Point

In his lectures on poetry, Hegel defined three ideal situations from which one can develop an epic story.[171] In this context, the term epic specifies one of the two main categories that differ from drama. Derived from Hegel's explanations, these initial situations are considered ideal for epic films: the first arises through war, warlike circumstances, or a natural disaster. These events can affect an entire nation, or at least a community, a social,

---

171 Cf. Szondi 1965, p. 141; 1987, p. 84

ethnic or religious group. Consequently, bravery is an essential characteristic of the characters of an epic story. In the first of these forms, warlike circumstances or catastrophes of any kind make it possible to portray a variety of situations and courageous acts in response to particular historical conditions. Almost all war movies and doomsday thrillers operate along with this pattern. Iconic examples in American film history related to this 'ideal situation' are BIRTH OF A NATION (D.W. Griffith, USA 1915) or GONE WITH THE WIND (Fleming, USA 1939). More recent productions in this regard are INDEPENDENCE DAY (Emmerich, USA 1996), DAY AFTER TOMORROW (Emmerich, USA 2004), THE DEER HUNTER (Cimino, USA 1978), THE WILD BUNCH (Peckinpah, USA 1969), REDACTED (De Palma, USA/CAN 2007), but as well STAR WARS (Lucas, USA 1977) and all its sequels or GAME OF THRONES (Benioff & Weiss, USA 2011–2019).

In the second form, which Hegel describes as 'ideal', the plot can develop in line with a biography. In the poetic and metaphorical design of a person, a character can evolve and change - or being observed - in reaction to events and the course of time. Consequently, the chosen situations to be included in the plot can happen across time and space and don't have to be any longer a causal chain of events. The central figure connects all elements. The life story of this character also expresses the theme of the movie. Examples include MOLIÈRE (Mnouchkine, F 1978) and LAWRENCE OF ARABIA (Lean, UK 1962) THE LAST TYCOON (Kazan, USA 1976), SPARTACUS (Kubrick USA 1960), ORLANDO (Potter, UK/R/I/F/NL 1992), EVITA (Parker, USA 1996), JACKIE (Larraín, USA/CHI/F/D 2016), and more.

The third option allows arranging an allegoric search: A metaphoric narration sets the inner world of the character, which is placed in a dialectic relationship with the outer world. Thus, one replaces the conflict by contrasting both areas. In such films, the main character is confronted with their desires, dreams and/or fears. Accordingly, they face an antagonist who incarnates their doubts or anxieties. The reality of everyday life can be confronted with an imaginary reality. A situation that replaces the conflict within the epic and open form results from the dichotomy and friction of the antagonistic elements of the inner and outer world. One such example is HIROSHIMA MON AMOUR (Resnais, F 1959): a movie about war and peace, love and death, pain and loss, hope and oblivion. It reflects on the impossibility of romantic love in the aftermath of a total catastrophe. Other films in which an allegorical search is central, are Das Cabinet des Dr Caligari (Wiene, D 1920), Geheimnisse einer Seele [Secrets of a Soul] (Pabst, D 1926) - Det Sjunde Inseglet [The Seventh Seal] (Bergman, S 1957), Le Enfants du Paradis (Carné, F 1945) and La Belle et La Bête (Cocteau, F 1946), Giuletta degli Spiriti (Fellini, I 1965), Goya [Goya or the Hard Way to Enlightenment] (Wolf, GDR 1971), Табор уходит в небо [The Queen of the Gypsies] (Loteanu, USSR 1977); Stalker (Andrei Tarkovsky, USSR 1979).

  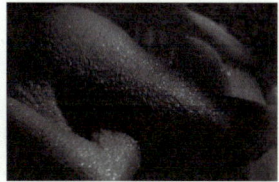

Fig. 17: La Belle et La Bete   Fig. 18: Giuletta degli Spiriti   Fig. 19: Hiroshima Mon Amour

Movies of this category are about seemingly everyday situations, at the explicit level. They reflect on or portray a particular chain of historical circumstances that inflict the life of one or more figures. It can be a period of stagnation, decadence, fear, paranoia, or restriction, or the utopia of complete happiness, a summer somewhere with friends or alone. These films sketch the lives of ordinary people. These figures are experiencing ups and downs, incidents or accidents, dreams and disappointments, presented in exemplary characters, as we can observe in movies by Andrei Tarkovsky, Eric Rohmer, Agnes Varda, Konrad Wolf, Věra Chytilová, Deepa Mehta, Sergei Parajanov or Andrey Zvyagintsev, to name a few. Films like Greed (Stroheim, USA 1924), La Notte (Antonioni, I/F 1961), I Vitelloni (Fellini, 1953) or Довлатов [Dovlatov] (German, RU/PL/SRB 2018) introduce the lives of others at a significant period of their life. Aristotle wrote that the epic narrative should amaze and entertain.[172] Carrière, for example, writes that he watches I Vitelloni again and again. In his opinion, there

---

172 Hegel 2003, p. 134–143

is no more complicated script than this. Ordinary people in everyday situations are introduced to us, nothing at all extraordinary happens, yet it is a captivating film.

Prelude and Prologue, Inversion and Framing

A prelude is an optional feature within film dramaturgy. One can compare it to a prologue and apply it in a variety of combinations. One should arrange it as a complete sequence. With its help, the interest of the audience is directed to a specific moment, character and/or fact. Basically, it prepares for the main plot.

Another optional element is that of 'inversion'. In literature, inversion is a technique that refers to the mythological or artistic ideal of justice, morality, perfection and the harmonious state of man at a time that is not precisely specified. Inversion negates time as determinable. With a dramatic sequence as provided by the technique of inversion, a situation can be represented that took place in the past, whose goal or topic, however, is directed into the future. It represents not an actual need, but rather a projection or utopia.[173] Such a revaluation of time leads the imagination of man. With the opportunities of art, a timeless ideal of a society that contains paradisian moments can be integrated into the experienced present and hence cause a confrontation or conflict like situation.[174] One can adapt this literary technique for film dramaturgy. Thus, a sequence can be positioned before the main action begins, although it occurs at a later moment within the story (again). An inversion thus determines the perspective of the viewer. It invites the audience to follow the developing events initiated by this first sequence. It, therefore, serves the participatory effect.[175] One example using this technique is STERNE [STARS] (Wolf, GDR 1959), another ROTATION (Staudte, 1949). More familiar to the readership might be THE USUAL SUSPECTS (Singer, USA/G 1995) that also begins with an inversion. The title sequence tunes in to a situation that takes place at night near the sea. An intertitle informs about place and time: San Pedro, California – last

---

173 Lotman 1977, p. 21, p. 335
174 Aristoteles & Schmitt 2008, chapter 24, a10–a20, p. 337
175 Cf. Stutterheim & Kaiser 2011, p. 107/108; Truffaut 2007, p. 64

night.[176] The film begins with an inversion. The opening shot is determined by a cinematic contrast that immediately creates tension. Shots of the dark water surface, on which isolated lights sparkle, are followed by a close-up of a flame. The central character sets a matchbox on fire. This figure (Gabriel Byrne) lights a cigarette and sets a circle of fuel on the fire. The progress of the flame is interrupted by someone, whom Byrne's character greets as Keyser (Kevin Spacey). These two men have a short conversation. The situation (the inversion) ends with the murder of Byrne's character. This situation is the moment of catastrophe within the explicit thriller plot, which takes place in the fifth act. But it's no longer shown in full length since this moment has already been introduced in the very beginning, before the otherwise chronologically told story.

Another example is INSIDE MAN (Lee, USA 2006). The inversion, as arranged for this movie, works as a variation of the prelude. The main actor (Clive Owen) introduces himself and addresses the audience directly. 'My name is Dalton Russel.'[177] For this prologue, dialogue sentences are combined, which that the character speaks in different situations that happen later in the course of the movie.

The sentence 'Pay strict attention to what I say because I choose my words carefully, and I never repeat myself,'[178] Dalton Russel directs to the audience. With precisely this sentence, the main character turns to the hostages held in the bank, which happens a little later, in the first act. One can detect several references here. The figure breaks through the fourth wall and is established as the central figure. This figure also incarnates a principle, at the collective level, of implicit dramaturgy. At this level, the story tells about justice and acts against racism.

The monologue continues after the introductory sequence. Author Russel Gurwitz and director Spike Lee play with conventions at the beginning of the film, and in this short monologue, they answer all the genre requirements of a thriller. They make the audience curious as to how this perfect bank robbery will be executed.

---

176 Bachtin 1986
177 S. Lee, USA 2006, 00:44 min
178 Ibid., 1:26 min

I told you my name. That's the 'who'. The 'where' could most readily be described as a prison cell. But there is a vast difference between being stuck in a tiny cell and being in prison. The 'what' is easy. Recently I planned and set in motion events to execute the perfect bank robbery. That's also the 'when.' As for the 'why', beyond the obvious financial motivation, it's exceedingly simple. Because I can. Which leaves us only with the 'how'. And therein, as the Bard would tell us, lays the rub.[179]

The last line refers to performative art and its traditions. In the course of the film, it will also become apparent that Dalton Russel doesn't reveal everything here.

Since this film qualifies as a postmodern film and a more detailed analysis would take up too much space here, it is only mentioned here to explain the principle of inversion.

Another opportunity to give a film a unique form allows the use of the technique of framing. This narrative technique emerges from the tradition of framing narratives and theatre plays employing a play-within-the-play structure, as in Shakespeare's *A Midsummer Night's Dream*,[180] *The Taming of the Shrew*[181] as "framed play", or *Hamlet*[182] being an "insert play". When using framing, two different levels of the narrative correlate. Tradition offers various possibilities. Framing narratives can be arranged, for example, as a realistic or introductory non-fiction commentary to a fictional main story. With framing, one can also refer to a past event which influences the course of the main action. In film, one can create an alienation effect similar to that of epic theatre by the use of an off-comment. Hence, one can arrange a situation in which a characters steps out of the scene and speaks directly to the audience, commenting on their case or informing about a fact related to the action. Examples here are EARTH (Mehta, 1998), AMADEUS (Forman, USA/F 1984) or VARGTIMMEN (Bergman, S 1968).

During the title sequence, which shows as titles on black, one hears Bergman and his team preparing the filming. VARGTIMMEN starts with a prologue scene, in which the main character (Liv Ullmann) addresses the audience directly. She sits at a table that dominates the scenery. She talks into the camera, to an imagined vis-a-vis and her text begins with 'No. I have nothing more to tell. I gave

---

179 S. Lee, USA 2006, 1: 35 min
180 Shakespeare, n.y.
181 Ibid.,
182 Ibid.

you the diary.'[183] She talks about her husband Johan (Max von Sydow) and an event they experienced there. This short introductory monologue establishes a secret. At the same time, it operates with contrast, as the character remembers happiness as well as a discomfort that turns into ever-increasing fear. She asks us a series of questions, some of them contradictory.[184] What she describes here to her imaginary counterpart is pictured again in the exposition. In the course of the action, her character is shown both as a participant and as an observer. The film ends with her turning again directly to her imaginary counterpart, the audience. The questions she asks herself in this final situation and addresses to us, invites us to reflect on what has happened. Nevertheless, these are open questions for which the author/direct does not provide an answer. It is up to us, every single member of the audience, to find a solution to her question. Bergman gave hints and logical strands, enabling us to do so by thinking about what we heard and what we were able to see and understand. In this way, the film has an open end, even though both the plot of the inner narration and of the framing come to a conclusion.

The Incident to Start the Action

The conflict is replaced by an incident to start the action. One can distinguish conflict and such an incident as follows: a conflict is triggered by the main character(s) or someone close to them, for example by misconduct that was of such magnitude that it has dangerous consequences. With an incident, neither the main character nor of those drawn as being close to them have influence on, or are to blame for what happens. Such incident have an effect on the situation in which the main character finds themselves forced to act. BLIND CHANCE (Kieślowski, PL 1987 (1981)) is a movie telling about incidents; they can culminate towards a catastrophe, as in LIFE ACCORDING TO AGFA (Dayan, ISR 1993) and GAME OF THRONES (Benioff & Weiss, USA 2011–2019). Everything can, explicit, follow an attempt for a new start, as in THE SHINING (Kubrick, UK/USA 1980), or caused by war as in IVAN'S CHILDHOOD (Andrei Tarkovsky, USSR 1961). An event forces characters into struggles for survival: EUROPA, EUROPA

---

183 Bergman 1968 2:27 min
184 Ibid. 1h 27 min

(Agnieszka Holland, G/F/PL 1990, a political confrontation gives THE DAY OF THE JACKAL (Zinnemann, UK/F 1973) its outset. An incident can be a catastrophe of any kind; or just caused by curiosity or portraying a moment in time as in Fellini's I VITELLONI (Fellini, I 1953). Independently of the chosen form, such a story emanates from a theme, a meaning.

Ideally, an action is triggered by an event that drastically influences the situation of the protagonist(s). This change can manifest itself when it affects those portrayed. This moment can imply a moment in which the protagonist must be remodified: The life of the main character may have been shaken up for some time - like that of the teacher who pretends to be a writer and gets the chance of a paid retreat in Kubrick's THE SHINING. There is also the traumatised detective/murderer in SHUTTER ISLAND who might be cured with the help of role play. In Иваново Детство [IVAN'S CHILDHOOD] (Andrei Tarkovsky, USSR 1961), it is Ivan, who loses his mother in the war and spies on her murderers. In THE HOURS (Daldry, USA/UK 2002) it is Virginia Woolf who takes her own life, but the book she writes shortly before her suicide inspires other women who come after her to master their lives. All of these stories are metaphors told as individual fates.

The particular event triggering the action may result from a process, which began sometime before the moment at the start of the movie. Hence, it impacts the life of the main character in particular. As in EUROPA, EUROPA (Holland, G/F/PL 1990), the film tells the story of a teenage Jew who flees from the Nazis to survive. A young man volunteers for the US Army during the Iraq war to finance his university education in REDACTED (De Palma, USA/CAN 2007). In GAME OF THRONES (Benioff & Weiss, USA 2011–2019) the behaviour of the king and the queen disrupt the order of an entire society and create chaos and war.

The Anchor: the 'Essential Meaning' and the 'Point of Convergence'

The dramaturgical concept of an open form culminates in the essential meaning ['*Bedeutungsfazit*'[185]] as the unifying element. Thus, every

---

185 Klotz 1980, p. 112

segment of the movie, every sequence, dialogue, the visual and sound design, become interrelated. Central to the explicit level of modern dramaturgy is to establish a situation equivalent to the *anagnorisis*, the *'moment of recognition'*. One can compare the concept of these two interrelated aspects with that of the central perspective, which also has a fix-point to which everything is aligned, but in geometry, there are also construction forms of perspective working with more than one vanishing point. For a modern drama composed as an open form, one can define this equivalent as a *vanishing point* or, more useful, as a *'point of convergence'*. This point centres the human gaze. From this position, the human gaze is directed towards an event. One can understand the vanishing point as a metaphorical eye. As the sketch below demonstrates, the 'vanishing point' and stabilises all elements.

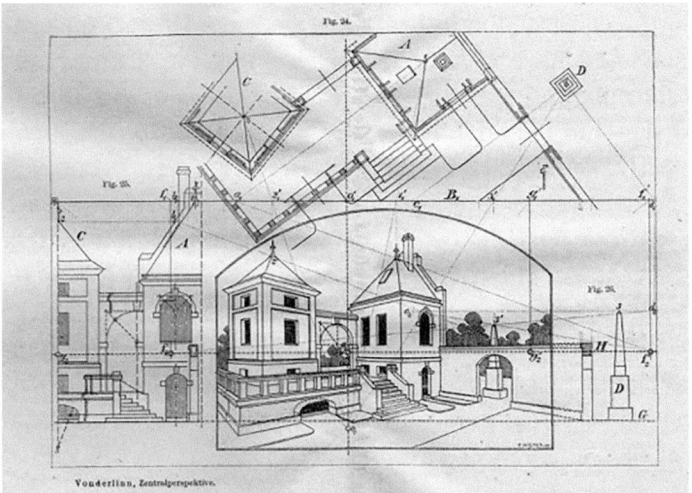

Fig. 20: Central Perspective, by Vonderlinn

SHUTTER ISLAND can serve here as an example to demonstrate this dramaturgical means. In the scene where the doctor explains the anagram to the main character, going with the names Andrew/Teddy, it becomes clear that everything that has happened on the explicit level so far has been a role play. This scene paces all events into a new relation.

Fig. 21: Point of   Fig. 22: Confrontation of   Fig. 23: Shot through
Convergence   Perspectives   the Layers

This situation represents the 'moment of recognition' and hence establishes the vanishing point of this plot. At the explicit level, the author/director gives information about the situation in which the main character finds himself. On the implicit level, the audience finds references about the approach of the author/director and the dramaturgical pattern used in the film. Accordingly, it can readjust its view of what is happening and its conclusions. From this situation, which reveals the motif, the theme and here also the construction of history, it becomes (better) understandable which characters have which function(s) within the chain of events, and why. In some films, the situation symbolising the 'moment of recognition' will also signal to the attentive viewer which aspect of the sophisticated theme a particular character represents. In SHUTTER ISLAND, this situation reveals that two perspectives that are distinct from each other overlap and meet in that moment: that of the detective, who acts out as Teddy; and that of the doctors, who try to heal the figure of Andrew hidden behind or inside the Teddy-character.

By creating a character that can change, it is also possible to include a wide range of further elements and a broad group of characters in the cinematic narrative. Each character functions within the overall dramaturgy. The effect of a film/film or narrative-performative work is influenced by the artistic design, regardless of the style, genre or medium of distribution involved.

Individual and Public Story Lines

It is characteristic of modern dramaturgy to structure a narrative over two corresponding levels. This technique supports the logical texture of a 'scenic narrative' and makes it possible to achieve an alienating effect. An appropriate dramaturgical structure allows the audience to recognise the dialectic of the circumstances and the state of the world causing the action, and which determines the character's behaviour. On the explicit level, the story of a particular person or group is told. This form of composition also results in the narrative thread of the individual. With the help of personal stories one can create typical situations and the resulting processes. Thus, one, author/directors and audience alike, can understand how the characters act in situations that could have happened to others as well. Consequently, a collective or 'public' thread is related to this.[186]

Such collective level results from circumstances the group that the protagonist(s) represents and to which he belongs. Their environment is defined by specific politic, ethnic, social, cultural, regional, or religious criteria. In modern drama or film, the family no longer necessarily forms the nucleus of coexistence. The experience and aftermath of existential events in the early 20th century initiated Modernity and a radically different approach to the world and its representation. Historical events, such as the Russian Revolution (1905–1907), World War I (1914–1918), the October Revolution (1917), as well as the Spanish Flu (1918–1920), destroyed the illusion that belonging to a family would guarantee a peaceful future for either the individual or the community. Hence, in Modern Art, the individual is no longer bound to a family, a region or religion, and status is no longer relevant either.[187] The individual is understood as a member of a group, community or representative of a state. The individual characters are designed accordingly, as are the rules within which they move. The concept of such belonging to a community forms the background for the principle of the public or collective level of narration. This principle represents the circumstances with which the character(s) are confronted. Accordingly, the plot, the film narration, can also contain moments of only implicit impact on plot and the protagonist(s). Such situations illustrate that the characters in films of open form or modern approach don't have to be in (dramatic) control or influence over events. These can be moments of social, political or historical relevance. These impact upon the unfolding action and contribute to the representation of the theme. All these aspects can be arranged unambiguously or metaphorically. Thus, this dramaturgical means makes

---

186 Klotz 1980, pp. 101–103
187 Cf. Hornby 1986, pp. 33–35

it possible to narrate fates that result from a unique and fundamental situation as *pars pro toto*.[188]

One interesting example, in which this connection of individual fate and the challenges a social group or community faces is presented, is BRASSED OFF (Herman, UK 1996). In this film, a group of different characters play a part within the film narration. All acting persons are connected, in one way or another, with the Grimley Brass Band. Their activities, as the city itself, depend on the regional coal mine. Central is the figure Danny (Pete Postlethwaite), accompanied by an ensemble. In particular, the bandleader Danny and his son Phil (Steven Tompkinson), personify the struggle and dreams of a family under such circumstances. Also, each role within the ensemble represents an individual story, which respectively allows a different angle on the overall plot.

Historical circumstances create a conflict-like situation. Designed as a cinematic conflict, a montage intertwines a rehearsal of the brass band and a meeting of the mine management. This situation escalates when the band-leader suffers a coughing attack.

Anagnorisis and peripeteia are arranged in a similar montage. The band plays in the semi-finals of the national brass band competition. The concert is edited parallel to the ballot about dismissal or strike. At the end of this scene, the brass band qualifies, but the colliery is about to be closed resulting from the ballot. Consequently, from a dramaturgical point of view, Danny, the band-leader, collapses on the street. The ambulance rescues him.

Embedded in the final concert of the national competition that takes place in the Albert Hall is the moment of the conclusion of the plot, adequate to 'catastrophe' in classic drama. The brass band wins, and this enables, within the dramaturgical construction as well as the logic of the explicit action, the band-leader to give a speech. The political situation can be expressed in this emotional situation. Through the representation of individual stories in such construction collective experience can be expressed; as such of the culture of brass bands which have been at the heart of the British working class and its culture for centuries.[189]

---

188 Eisenstein 1923; Michalski 1994, p. 66
189 Brass Bands are a tradition of communities around local industries in the UK
      since the early 19th century, with competitions locally and nationally; it provided

Ivan's Childhood

Andrei Tarkovsky's movie ИВАНОВО ДЕТСТВО [Ivan's Childhood] (Andrei Tarkovsky, USSR 1961) is another excellent example to explain this principle. A broad personage accompanies the character going with the name Ivan. The war influences the individual fate of every one of these characters. The war and its traumatic effect is the overall theme and connect every element of the movie. Every one of these characters represents different effects which war, in general, has on human beings.

Ivan's motive is to take revenge on those representing the murder of his mother. He is extraordinarily courageous and strong, risking his life all the time. Ivan has no illusion of getting his mother back. His future lies within the community, the army unit that replaces the family. His activities ensure the future of his community. He succeeds corresponding to the pattern of a dramatic hero, on his 'individual level', to gain little victories over the enemy. His activities help in achieving the overthrow of the Nazi-dictatorship at the end of the movie. The young character (Nikolay Burlaev), is different from boys his age. The directing of this actor is as precise as his performance.

And moreover, the positioning of the character, the arrangement of the scenery and the cinematographic style create an effect, which keeps us, the spectator, at a distance although we empathise with Ivan. The movie begins with a dream sequence contrasting peace and war. The sunny dream landscape of the beginning marks a 'paradisiacal state', which since Ancient drama one considers as the ideal starting point for a dramatic narration.[190] A paradisiacal state does not mean the utopia of perfect happiness; it describes the best possible everyday-life situation a character can be situated within.[191] The terrifying moment ending the dream, and waking the Ivan of the narrated present, tells us about the central character's background and his motivation. To connect the prelude-like vision with the plot and

---

in particular working class communities in the northern part of England with social and cultural identity. The coal mining industry was the powerhouse of England, with 1920 over a Million employees, 1960 600thausand, 1980 still about 250thausand reduced to 49thausand in 1990, Statistica, 2018

190 Hegel 2003, pp. 134–137
191 Cf. Hegel 1971, p. 295/296

thus enrich the implicit level, the next in the next scene, Tarkovsky shows Ivan leaving the place he slept. In this transition sequence, Ivan walks through a war-torn landscape. The destroyed windmill and farmer's tools symbolise the effect the war has on all areas of life — this picture, in particular, associates devastation, hunger, and death.

Fig. 24: Ivan and his   Fig. 25: Ivan's Mother   Fig. 26: Devastation
Mother

The novel, which Tarkovsky adapted for his movie, attracted him for several reasons. One feature he was particularly intrigued by was the main character's young age:

> A third thing moved me to the bottom of my heart: the personality of the young boy. He immediately struck me as a character that had been destroyed, shifted off its axis by the war. Something incalculable, indeed, all the attributes of childhood, had gone irretrievably out of his life. And the thing he had acquired, like an evil gift from the war, in place of what had been his own, was concentrated and heightened within him. His character moved me by his intensely dramatic quality, which I found far more convincing than those personalities which are revealed in the gradual process of human development, through situations of conflict and clashes of principle.[192]

Starting from these thoughts, Tarkovsky uses the principle of the cinematic conflict and visual dramaturgy to transform these contrasting situations into a dramatic process. Thus, echoing the classic conflict. Tarkovsky invented a new style of metaphoric visual narration within the cinematic practice. His aesthetic approach enables him to intertwine the individual and the public level of narration through distinctive metaphoric referentiality. In such a situation, to be understood here, equivalent to the anagnorisis, Ivan looks through a book and reacts to Albrecht Dürer's engraving *The Apocalyptic Riders*:

---

192 Tarkovsky 1986, p. 17

Fig. 27: Ivan saw one of them

Fig. 28: Albrecht Dürer: Die Apokalyptischen Reiter

"Boy, look at that. Are these Germans?" "Yes. It is an old engraving." "They're Fritz all the same. This one, on a horse, all skin and bones. I saw one just like him on a motorcycle. Look, they're trampling the people here too." "It's just someone's imagination." "Imagination. I know them. Is he a Fritz too?" "He is a German Doctor or writer." "They have no writers. I saw them burning books in a square. They poured gasoline on them and set them on fire. There was soot in the air for a week."[193]

With this sequence, Tarkovsky applies the theme in a metaphoric situation. Since the Ivan of the explicit narration cannot have been in one of the German cities in 1933 at the time of the 'Bücherverbrennung' [book burning], he now embodies the metaphoric observer of the war and all crimes of Nazi Germany.

The initial construction of Ivan's Childhood mirrors in Klimov's Иди и смотри [Come and See] (Klimov, USSR 1985), for example. Martin Scorsese refers to Ivan's Childhood in his movie Shutter Island. Here, the protagonist was involved in freeing the Concentration Camp of Dachau and survived but traumatised. One can interpret Teddy/Andrew (Leonardo di Caprio) as the American equivalent to Galtsev (Yevgeni Zharikov), one of the main characters in Ivan's Childhood. On the implicit level, references become obvious.

---

193 Cf. Stutterheim 2015, p. 222

Fig. 29: SHUTTER ISLAND   Fig. 30: SHUTTER ISLAND

Fig. 31: IVAN'S CHILDHOOD   Fig. 32: IVAN'S CHILDHOOD

Heroic Anti-Heroes

The plot can be presented by the action of the main character, a pair, or an ensemble. As in all dramatic art, characters serve the action; they are composed and impersonated by actors who develop characteristics for their persona and situated in relation to the overall composition of the work.[194] Roles in modern and even more in postmodern films, or those of a 'stylish style', as Bordwell[195] labels it, often represent a principle. As a personification of a character, they have to resemble human beings. These principles are true for cinema movies as well as for contemporary 'high-quality TV' or 'auteur-series'.[196] These characters should be incorporations of 'people who you either wish you were like or glad you are not.'[197]

---

194 cf. Stutterheim 2015, p. 143 et sequ.
195 Bordwell, 2006, p. 115
196 Cf. Dreher 2014
197 Owen, 2004, p. 108

Characters that we are introduced to in films of these categories are often described as passive or anti-heroes. The distinction between heroes and passive figures or anti-heroes in film theory derives from a time when movies were part of an entertainment industry supporting either capitalist interests to motivate the audience to drive the economy back into full flow; or, as it was in Stalin's Soviet Union, to motivate the audience to participate actively in socialist campaigns. In both cases, active heroes were required; and flâneurs, complacent, timid, or shy personalities negatively connoted.

Characters presented in modern films are no longer bound to a religious, a God-given, and a total or idealised order. They act within a social or historical situation. These new characters are no longer of royal blood, higher ranks, or a noble person. The individual is a member of a community he/she may have chosen or come to be associated with due to particular circumstances. For example, by being a specialist hired to establish communication with aliens (ARRIVAL, Villeneuve, USA 2016) or to act as a spy against German Nazi Soldiers (IVAN'S CHILDHOOD). Human rights replace religious orthodoxy or royal orders.

In modern dramaturgy, protagonists as well as side characters, can make mistakes, hesitate, lose track, and re-orientate themselves. Alternatively, the main character can be split into two or more figures up to an ensemble to give its inner self, inner conflict or its richness of character traits, its male and female parts, or other ways to define a personality, a personification. Since every sequence in a modern dramaturgy is connected to or based on the overall theme, a character can change their behaviour by reacting to the challenge of the moment.

A modern protagonist acts on the situation, at the moment. Emotional outbursts are allowed when these are supporting the action and/or an understanding of the theme and the moment of recognition. One can present characters as driven by suppressed dreams, unconscious energies, fears or delusions. They are like others around them, but due to a particular event, moment or characteristic, they are an example representing and thus embodying the traits of a social group. That makes them more than an impersonation of one individual. Hence, children can also be protagonists, as Ivan (Nikolay Burlyaev) in IVAN'S CHILDHOOD (Andrei Tarkovsky, USSR 1961), or Salomon (Marco Hofschneider) in EUROPA, EUROPA (Agnieszka

Holland, D/F/PL 1990), Chuyia (Sarala Kariyawasam) in Water (Mehta, CAN/IND 2005).

A demonstration of a state of mind is one way to illustrate the concept of the impossibility of proposing a satisfying solution to the challenge of the social and mental situation of the contemporary world.[198] Consequently, interpersonal dialogues are no longer the primary or the only tool to inform the audience about context and motivation.

In modern dramaturgy, at least three main categories of protagonists emerged.

The Central Self

One opportunity to align a fragmented narration along a protagonist is by applying the principle of a central self.[199] Such a protagonist can reflect on the action he/she is part of. In movies, a central self represents a person who is new to the situation or an outsider becoming involved. Implicit, this person enables the audience to orientate itself in a complex narrative. A 'central self' embodies a particular approach to the theme and hence, to the overall story.

This technique allows incorporating a subjective process into the action, to elaborate thoughts and sentience, which otherwise would require tools to be expressed, like a letter, an email, or any form of a messaging. Alternatively, a monologue could voice these. The composition of central self as the main character allows addressing the audience directly as a narration out of the off. The central self is a figure that plays a leading part in the action without being involved in the cause of it.[200] They can ask questions, express their amazement or comment on events. As in most cases, various examples can be mentioned here. The central self can be a character designed like Elle (Emmanuelle Riva) in Hiroshima Mon Amour (Resnais, F 1959). Margarete Duras wrote the dialogues between her, Elle, and Lui (Eiji Okada) as a couple talking to each other in a way as if they are talking to themselves. Lui is the opposite character to Elle. He is representing the

---

198 Emrich 2014
199 Cf. Brinckmann 1981
200 Brecht 1977, p. 409

male aspect, the object of love and desire, but as well the soldier and thus one aspect of war. Lui is a symbol of infidelity. As an incarnation of Elle's first love, he would not be allowed to fall for French women, and she not to love a German soldier. As Lui from Hiroshima, he is married, a former soldier. He is representing as well – from her point of view – the other. Some of the dialogue texts of Elle have the characteristics and expression of monologues, reflecting her thoughts and emotions, directed towards the audience. The screenplay written by Marguerite Duras is a poetic reflection on the theme, of historical events, and how these manifest as trauma, as memories and mourning in Elle.

A central self, who is leading the action and commenting on the events unfolding is the character going by the name of 'Verbal' Roger Kint, or, as one recognises later, Keyser Soze (Kevin Spacey). His off-narration fills the gaps, gives information, and allows time shifts in THE USUAL SUSPECTS (Singer, USA/G 1995). And, he symbolises a version of an 'unreliable narrator' in a genre movie, as it will be discussed later.

The character Salieri in AMADEUS (Forman USA/F 1984) looks back on his rivalry with Mozart. He accuses himself of having killed his rival. Thus, Forman lets Salieri tell his story to a priest visiting him in his cell in the mental institution. We watch the priest listening to Salieri's monologues to God. Those sequences, in which Salieri comments on events and tells about his jealousy, his admiration for Mozart's musical talent, and his disgust with Mozart as a person. These interludes bring the audience at a distance to the personal narrative. The audience is asked to observe the situation, not to immerse fully into the story.

The character going by the name of Tyrion Lannister (Peter Dinklage) in GAME OF THRONES (Benioff & Weiss, USA 2011–2019) is another variation of a 'central self'. This character is introduced as an outsider, observer, and commentator on the action. He represents a philosopher and 'master of rhetoric', although from a cynical distance. This Tyrion is always striving for his well-being and survival. This trait is woven into his dialogue regularly and confirmed again, especially at the end of the series. Therefore, he can reflect on the events unfolding, and by doing so, his figure supports the audience, not only the character he is talking to, with additional information or explanations. This theory that he is a central figure is supported by the fact that Tyrion Lannister is the figure acting in most of the episodes – in 67 out of 86[201], more than any other character. And this Tyron-character is the one of the few who crosses most topographically diverted storylines. To cover his dramaturgical function, he needs this attractive character trait and touching fate. Although of short stature and cheeky, the Tyrion character is appealing to the audience, not to underestimate the excellent acting by Peter Dinklage to give this figure a consistent, believable appearance.[202]

In THE GHOST WRITER (Polański, UK/F/D 2010), the central self is of similar design. He, the character of the Ghost (Ian McGregor), becomes the new ghost writer for a former premier minister (Pierce Brosnan). The Ghostwriter represents an author who is designed as a person of naïve curiosity which hence enables an analytical drama to unfold. All other characters, situations, events, as well as the proceeding narrative threads, are composed as if seen from his perspective. By being designed as a person, who is in a position to asks questions, comment on events, and tell others about their thoughts and findings, the Ghost is as a modern version of the central self.

Other examples in this context are movies such as ERIN BROCKOVICH (Soderbergh, USA 2000) and WATER (Mehta, CAN/IND 2005) as well as POLISSE (Maïwenn, F 2011). In ERIN BROCKOVICH, the main character (Julia Roberts), after which the film is titled, works for a solicitor. Throughout the action, we observe how she becomes concerned with a particular case, which looks banal at first. She, the outsider, underestimated by everyone, becomes the person able to gather vital information to discover an environmental scandal and enabling a successful prosecution of the concern behind this. This central character directs the audience's view on the situation, its political and social context. The action led by the character representing Erin Brockovich is an untypical personal story, which has in itself universal aspects. Through her work and the unfolding events, we are introduced to other exemplary stories representing different people and their fates in contemporary America. In POLISSE, the character through which this connecting becomes established is a photographer. The action begins with the photographer going

---

by the name Melissa (Maïwenn) appointed to take photographs of the everyday life of a child protection unit of a police station in Paris. As a photographer, her character can be the observing and stirring outsider but interacting with the ensemble. A variation of this is the main character that Deepa Mehta developed for WATER. A very young widow, Chuyia (Sarala Kariyawasam), still a child, is the newcomer to a house, where the widows have to live separated from society. She is too young to be like them, but technically, she is a widow like they are. By showing how this girl finds her place, gets to know and questions all the rules, rituals, and individual stories of each of the other widows imprisoned together, Mehta draws a kaleidoscope of the situation of women at a particular time in Indian history.

In all of these films, the central self is directing comments which either lead to other characters or as a variation of a monologue offstage.

A different example is the figure Alma (Liv Ullmann) in VARGTIMMEN [THE HOUR OF THE WOLF] as mentioned above. Her character addresses the audience directly, speaks to an imaginary vis-à-vis and reflects on the situation and events unfolding.

The Centre Figure [Mittelpunktfigur]

The Centre figure has some resemblance to the Central Self, although there are some features, which distinguish them from one another. Bertolt Brecht established the term. Brecht developed figures and stories from the rich tradition of theatre, which he developed according to experience in the contemporary world and the unfolding modern art.

In his plays, Brecht invited the audience to respond to events his characters is thrown into and have to deal with. These characters represent people from the edge of the society, poor people, farmer, worker, criminals, not heroic in the sense of classical drama yet typical for modern art. In the classic drama tradition, a hero is a member of a royal family, or since the middle of the 19th century, of a respected profession or social rank. Brecht defined the 'Mittelpunktfigur', which one can translate as 'centre figure', as the role of a person imitated who is part of a particular group that they represent. The event initiating the action is going to affect a group, a social commu- nity, or a political class. The centre figure is a member of the group and can be of any social status.[203] Such an incorporated person can be shown as affected in a particular way, hence developed as a metaphoric character. This principle allows the spectator to concentrate on the effect the event has on the group, which is represented by the centre figure's fate. To follow up on the characteristic introduced above, one can design the centre figure as a person who doesn't necessarily attract our emotional identification – like Mackie Messer [Mack the Knife] in Brecht's *Dreigroschenoper [Three Penny Opera]*.[204] Nevertheless, we develop an interest in this character who is shown as being primed by circumstances. The centre figure can be designed as an outsider in a social group, like Mack the Knife.

Consequently, such a character has to explain himself to other characters. This concept is similar to that of the central self. The feature which is distinct in principle is the opportunity given to a central figure to step out of the situation and to address the audience directly. The main feature of composing a centre figure is the given fact that one has to show how a person is experiencing a situation, for which he or she is neither prepared for nor warned against.

Salomon, the protagonist of EUROPA, EUROPA, is addressing the audience and commenting on his situation. Agnieszka Holland decided on an off-narration, which gives voice to Salomon's thoughts. Thus, the character can respond to events and act in contrast to the events unfolding. The story begins in 1939 in Poland with a pogrom and Nazi troops occupying the city. One sister murdered, the elder brother joining the resistance army. Salomon, as the youngest son, and his older brother, are sent away to make sure they will stay alive. On the explicit level, Salomon manages to survive by reacting to events he faces. As a teenager, who has to survive on his own, he finds himself confronted with a murderous regime and war. Accordingly, he is not acting heroically but survives. Every day anew. Surviving under such circumstances can be seen as heroic. By doing so, he expresses hope for the future. To enable the future of the community the character belongs to is the core dramaturgical feature for a hero in a classical drama. Holland uses irony to let the main character tell of his fate. In these situations, an alienation effect is achieved. The principle of

---

203 Brecht 1966c, p. 218
204 Brecht 1965

a center figure most often goes together with the aesthetic concept of the
"*V-Effekt*"– the 'alienation effect'.

The Open Ending

To end a film following the principles of the modern dramaturgy requires
artistic skills. The challenge is, to bring the primary storyline to an end
and to keep the ending open at the same time. Following the essential principles of film dramaturgy, one needs situations equivalent to catastrophe
and catharsis.[205] As mentioned already, the audience should be invited to
think about the film, to reflect on the action, characters, and succession
of events. Therefore a balance between the required ending and openness
needs to be achieved. Some examples may help to present a possible range
of open ends.

Openness can result from a surprising ending as it does in THE USUAL
SUSPECTS (Singer, USA/G 1995). This has a typical ending following the
genre conventions in the sense of a catastrophe/showdown. That is that of
the character of Dean Keaton (Gabriel Byrne) murdered at the end of the
task the team of criminals had to perform resulting from being blackmailed
by the much-feared figure introduced as Keyser Soze. The surprise and
consequent change of the perspective on everything that happened are triggered when it becomes evident that the character 'Verbal' is not disabled at
all. This character played a game with them and schemed with everyone.
That this intrigue aimed to get his revenge, as one may understand when
reflecting on the action from this new perspective, gives the ending also
the quality of a closure. Very similar is the construction of the conclusion
of THE SIXTH SENSE (Shyamalan, USA 1999). When it is revealed that the
child psychiatrist was dead all the time and different levels of reality and
imagination were combined, one has to reconsider the whole plot.

In movies which use the technique of framing, the characters comment
on the events, and most often, these characters invite us to take a position
on their matter. Thus, Alma in VARGTIMMEN [THE HOUR OF THE WOLF]
is searching for an explanation, asking her imaginary vis-à-vis questions,

---

205 Dreher 2014; Dreher & Akass 2010

admits by addressing this person that she has no additional information that might help to understand the situation and even fears for herself.

Related to this approach are movies which tell about an historical situation or a biography when reflecting the effect of the events in the future, which is the case in movies such as IVAN'S CHILDHOOD (Andrei Tarkovsky, USSR 1961), THE DEER HUNTER (Cimino, USA 1978), STALKER (Tarkovsky, USSR 1979), BRASSED OFF (Herman, UK 1996), EARTH (Mehta, 1998) and WATER (Mehta, CAN/IND 2005).

In LAWRENCE OF ARABIA (Lean, UK 1962), in the end, there is still the question to be answered by the spectator, asked in the prelude: Does he deserve a place in St Paul's Cathedral?

The conclusions of movies like SHUTTER ISLAND (Scorsese, USA 2010) or THE SHINING (Kubrick, UK/USA 1980) are less explicit. The audience has to interpret the end, which derives from visual elements, the implicit dramaturgy and its referentiality but not so much from the dialogues of the last scenes if there are any at all. Since both movies wrap a highly political topic in a genre story, the audience is invited to think more about the plot than the quality of the explicit structure.

Implicit Dramaturgy and Aesthetic

As introduced above, a dramaturgy for a modern and postmodern film not only focusses on a screenplay, written and spoken dialogues but the whole work in all of its aspects. For film dramaturgy, all levels of narration are equally of importance. The aesthetics of a movie are an essential part of the effect of a film. The audience is invited to see, hear, and think. Consciously as well as unconsciously references to the art of avant-garde films and those made in the 1920s and 1930s, as by Sergei Eisenstein, Fritz Lang, Erich von Stroheim, to name a few, are apparent – as these are for examples references to be found in the aesthetic design of GAME OF THRONES (Benioff & Weiss, USA 2011–2019)[206] to mention one contemporary example. In films, which one can define as modern or postmodern, poetic, cinematic, creative or following the principles of the open form, the audio-visual narration is complex. Modern film dramaturgy can, with the help of dramaturgical knowledge

---

206 Cf. Bonusmaterial Benioff & Weiss, USA 2016; Stutterheim, 2019

derived from the tradition of dramatic and cinematic narrative, enable and support filmmakers to create such complexity without creating confusion. Of crucial importance in this context is the design of the implicit dramaturgy.

Poetic Narration and the Spectator

Ideally, the dramaturgical structure of a modern, as well as a postmodern movie, is developed through several interconnected layers of narration. All elements must serve the theme and general plot of the particular work. Thus, the audience is invited into an act of interpretation, to read 'their' story within the given framework.

Modern and postmodern narratives address audiences who enjoy thinking for themselves.[207] Since the 1920s and especially since the Nouvelle Vague, many authors and directors have been working towards a *cinema of meaning*, as introduced in more detail below. The knowledge of the cinematic language and dramaturgical rules helps to design a touching and attractive movie, which attracts and invites the audience. Viewers today are skilled at understanding cinematic means and can thus easily follow a sophisticated and openly designed film.

> Through poetic connections feeling is heightened and the spectator is made more active. He becomes a participant in the process of discovering life, unsupported by ready-made deductions from the plot or ineluctable pointers by the author. He has on his disposal only what helps to penetrate to the deeper meaning of the complex phenomena represented in front of him. Complexities of thought and poetic visions of the world do not have to be thrust into the framework of the patently obvious. The usual logic, that of linear sequentiality, is uncomfortably like the proof of a geometric theorem.[208]

The dramaturgy of an open form emerges from the basic rules that have developed over time. On this basis, the possibilities for designing a work of art in modern dramaturgy are very diverse. Through a poetic form, the writer/director invites the audience to an active reception. Using their knowledge, supported by cultural memory[209] and traditions known to him/her, the viewer can interpret the work and relate it to their own experience.

---

207 Kahneman 2012; Rancière 2011; Stutterheim 2016; Stein 1935, p. 46/47
208 Tarkovsky 1986, p. 20
209 A. Assmann 2011; J. Assmann 2006, 2007, 2011

The production of a text of any kind, a work of art, a film, is a dynamic process in which many artistic and otherwise qualified people are involved.[210] In a professional and high quality produced film, the work which went into it, is hidden. It 'is likely a product, of changes induced by complex aesthetic, ethical, ideological, or pragmatic, mechanical decisions by the author and, for that matter, negotiations between the author and his or her environment.'[211] It is the vision and talent of the writer/directors and their team, through which the film attracts the audience, to surprise them, and emotionally touch them, when after some time the work will be released or distributed.

A Cinema of Meaning

During the early 1960s, players of *Nouvelle Vague* and authors of *Cahiers du Cinema* described the new, modern, open narrated movies as 'cinema of meaning'. Their discourse about cinema interacted with those of anthropology and literature studies as well as Lacan's approach to psychoanalysis and Althusser's concepts. Above all, Alain Resnais' L'ANNÉE DERNIÈRE À MARIENBAD [LAST YEAR IN MARIENBAD] (Resnais F 1961) has been discussed as initiating a 'Copernican Revolution' in Western cinema.[212] Contemporary cinema productions emerged from the theories of Bazin[213] and Barthes[214] as well as Pier Paolo Pasolini's essay about 'poetic cinema' accentuating 'meaning' concerning the modern.[215]

Movies directed by Antonioni, Resnais, or Tarkovsky, experimented with new narrative forms and thus encouraged their audience to interpret their work. The audience became a 'hero' themselves by replacing the dramatic hero. As 'cinema of meaning' can be identified the works of Federico Fellini, Miklós Jancsó, Jean-Marie Straub and Danièle Huillet, Jean-Luc Godard, Andrej Wajda, Krzysztof Zanussi, Krzysztof Kieślowski,

---

210 Cf. i.a. Carrière 1994; Danko 2005; Eisler 1975; Hecht 1979; Mamet 1991
211 Coelsch-Foisner 2005, p. vii
212 Brecht 1977
213 Bazin 2004; Bazin 1975
214 Barthes 1987
215 Bickerton 2009, p. 42

Agnes Varda, Jacques Tati, and Pier Paolo Pasolini. Inspired by new technical devices and the intellectual discourse of the time, these filmmakers challenged conventions in narration and aesthetics. For Jacques Rivette, incompleteness is the goal every director should strive to achieve. It is the strength of modern cinema.

Such 'cinema of meaning' was intended to create concreteness rather than illustrating it. The new cinema questions the reality, awakes in the audience more than simple acceptance, it creates a new realness or presents a new perspective on events and circumstances.[216] Their approach combines the concept of the 'absolute film'[217] and Brecht's dialectic theatre.[218] To achieve a materialist-sensual quality of a reflection on reality, directors began to develop a new artistic and poetic style. Hitchcock was an idol to many of them. He was much admired by *Cahier du Cinema* writers and in particular by François Truffaut.[219] Also, Tarkovsky's IVAN'S CHILDHOOD (Tarkovsky USSR 1962) inspired Godard and other filmmakers of the *Nouvelle Vague*. In all his films, Tarkovsky creates a poetic correspondence between reality and imagination. Among others, the poetry of his father Arseny Tarkovsky was of influence, which Andrei Tarkovsky transforms into a cinematic narrative,[220] next to artistic role models like Sergei Eisenstein or Vsevolod Pudovkin of the film tradition developed in the Soviet Union. 'Scenes, images, and levels of consciousness, as well as times, emerge or merge, drawing the reader into unfamiliar, shifting areas of awareness.'[221] Truffaut, Resnais, Varda, Chabrol and other directors who were associated with or influenced by the *Cahier du Cinema* wanted to touch the audience and make them think. They thus repeated the intentions of filmmakers from the period before the 1929 Depression, before the Second World War, dictatorships in Germany and the Soviet Union, the McCarthy era and others that imposed restrictions on the fields of art and film.

---

216 Comolli, Fairfax, & Comolli
217 Balázs 2001, p. 81 et sequ.
218 Brecht 1966d
219 Truffaut, Grafe, and Patalas 2007
220 Tarkovskii & Hunter-Blair
221 Ibid., p. 27

Films that follow an approach that invites the audience to think and interpret follow dramaturgical principles. Declaring such movies to be 'anti-' or 'non-' to an established conservative principle results from from the standpoint of society giving certain tenets a privileged status. Such a position is what the filmmakers of the Nouvelle Vague rebelled against. They rebelled against a situation resulting from the Second World War as earlier artists did already in reaction to World War I, thus initiating Modernism. Accordingly, one can say that in their modern and postmodern films, contemporary writer-directors react to and comment on a present situation. Consequently, they stand in the tradition of modern film and a *cinema of meaning*.

Metaphoric Narration and Cinematic Conflict

In modern and postmodern films or TV productions, the visual narration is of pre-eminent importance because of its metaphoric quality. Visual design and referentiality support the concept of elucidating and representing the theme, the essential meaning. Set design and props can be designed to underpin this aesthetic concept. Therefore they must be deliberately chosen. The scenery is more than a mise-en-scène. The visual narration can also convey aspects of an underlying idea for the movie as part of the implicit dramaturgy. Let me demonstrate this once again with the example of THE SHINING (Kubrick, UK/USA 1980). The topographical situation of the scene already has an inherent connotation and informs the developing action. The hotel is situated on top of the mountain. It is about to be closed for the winter season since extreme weather can occur. It is a welcome circumstance that the caretaker hired for the winter season is going to bring his family with him. They will keep him company. To be not alone over the winter is believed to be good for the productivity and mental health of the caretaker. These aspects are elements of explicit dramaturgy. But, on the implicit level, there is more. The top of the mountain is also the place to build a fortress or another building guaranteeing the outlook and also the power over the land below.[222] The mountain peak is equally a part of the world where the demons can enter the world of humans.[223]

---

222 Cf. Warnke, 1992, p. 45–62
223 Sachs, Badstübner, & Neumann, 1980, p. 90 - Daemonen

Moreover, in the movie, this hotel is situated in the Shining Mountains, an area where one of the most brutal civil wars against the Native Americans took place.[224] The topographical context, together with the musical leit-motif informs the implicit dramaturgy and the theme of the movie.[225] All this is supported by the design of the area around the hotel, such as the labyrinth, as well as the interior and costume design. The camera work, the editing, and of course the actors also contribute their part.

An excellent example of how music and visual narratives can create a cinematic conflict is the scene in BRASSED OFF (Herman, UK 1996) in which we observe the orchestra rehearse the *Concierto d'Aranjuez.*[226] That piece of music tells about love and death. As a cultural heritage, it also represents power and dependency. That this very concerto is performed is an implicit contribution to the actual situation that we observe at the explicit level of action.

The cinematography, acting, and editing serves that particular artistic approach. Suspense can emerge from the intended use of the visual-acoustic counterpoint, also known as cinematic or aesthetic conflict, as introduced in chapter one. One aspect of establishing an aesthetic conflict is sound design and music as part of the dramaturgical concept. It supports the rhythm, the pace, and is the peotic element of a work.

Activation of Space

Space is visible and concrete. One can change a place or the mise-en-scène, one can move in it or run away, walk, ride or drive; cross a landscape. People can cultivate and decorate a place. We are able to define space due to its physical existence and our experience of it as the physical environment, in which we orientate ourselves. The mise-en-scène provides orientation about the setting in which the events take place.

Consequently, in modern films, space gives the explicit dramaturgy its physical orientation, the connection to the audiences' experience of the

---

224 o.N., 1867
225 cf. Stutterheim 2015, p. 49–78
226 Herman, UK 1996, min 15–20; https://www.youtube.com/watch?v=zo8hIc7DpuE

world. Beyond that, a location can enrich the implicit dramaturgy when it is a place containing a meaning. Examples are, amongst others, the Three Gorges as a symbolic landscape for the time and culture of the Tang Dynasty in STILL LIFE (Zhangke CH 2006); the Mulholland Drive and its history for Lynch's movie of the same title, MULHOLLAND DRIVE (Lynch, USA 2001); the 'Zone' in STALKER (Tarkovsky USSR 1979) as a haunted post-war place.

Fig. 33: STILL LIFE (Zhangke)

Fig. 34: MULHOLLAND DRIVE (Lynch)

Fig. 35: STALKER (Tarkovsky)

On the other hand, implicit dramaturgy can give a meaning to places as well. As mentioned above, the specific characteristics of a modern film require designing a mise-en-scène, which transports a symbolic meaning and no longer has to be a naturalistic depiction of reality.

> It is crucial that *mise en scene*, rather than illustrating some idea, should follow life—the personalities of the characters and their psychological state. Its purpose must not be reduced to elaborating on the meaning of a conversation or action. Its function is to startle us with the authenticity of the actions and the beauty and depths of the artistic images—not by obtrusive illustration of their meaning.[227]

The location can be a landscape, building, or interior. Tarkovsky, for example, arranges for IVAN'S CHILDHOOD those sequences that take place at the army camp always as a stage-like situation. Thus, he highlights the artificiality of his movie, emphasising the performative character.

In GAME OF THRONES (Benioff & Weiss, USA 2011–2019), many situations are similarly composed. The Iron Throne, like all other thrones, is situated on a podium equivalent to a stage, which makes everyone in front of these reciprocally the audience. Throughout the series, many speeches are

---

227 Tarkovsky 1986, p. 25

given from various forms of rostrums.[228] For example, the parents observing their sons at the archery ground and commenting on their action[229], Theon Greyjoy (Alfie Allen) who delivers a speech to his troop in Winterfell[230], Walder Frey (David Bradley) addressing his people and guests at the Red Wedding[231] and Arya Stark (Maisie Williams) as Frey taking up this situation when she takes revanche.[232]

The landscape can represent the quality of a character, in dramaturgical terms. Examples are CAST AWAY (Robert Zemeckis, USA 2000), THE PERFECT STORM (Petersen, USA 2000), THE ICE STORM (A. Lee, USA 1997), and STALKER (Tarkovsky, 1979). In CAST AWAY, the island on which the main character Chuck Noland (Tom Hanks) lands after his plane crashes is arranged as the antagonist. The same is true for THE PERFECT STORM.

In Tarkovsky's STALKER, two different landscapes are central to the story. The first one is the area where the Stalker (Alexander L. Kaidanowski) and his family live. It is an industrial area, the colours bleached out. It represents the state of society. During the travel into the 'zone', the landscape becomes colourful, and birds are singing. But this landscape is also an antagonistic character. Indeed it is designed like a modern character. It can change its mind and the degree of its interaction. The Stalker is the mind reader of the 'zone', which also represents the utopia of the Free Will. Immanuel Kant defines the will's freedom as defined by both, the good and the evil.[233] Accordingly, the 'zone' can react to its visitors and their wishes and fears. It can be helpful or dangerous.

Scorsese applied a variation of this aesthetic principle for SHUTTER ISLAND when referencing M.C. Escher's drawings[234] of staircases leading only back to other stairs but never a way out. Scorsese applies such a reference at least twice. One is the situation in which both detectives enter

---

228 Stutterheim 2017, p. 47–49
229 GoT I-1
230 GoT II-06
231 GoT III-09
232 GoT VI-10
233 Cf. Kant, 2012, p.
234 MC Escher (1898–1972), was a Dutch graphic artist who became famous for his mathematical art which show impossible realities.

the main building to meet Dr Crowley (Ben Kingsley). The second scenery referencing Escher gives the fight scene in Tract C an additional impression of being trapped and results in the effect of uncanniness.

A landscape or its appearance, as well as weather events, can also be designed as a metaphor for the 'Seelenlandschaft' [soul landscape] of the main character(s). One can translate *Seelenlandschaft* as a reflection on an inner state of mind of the main character. In implicit dramaturgy, topography transformed into mise-en-scène corresponds to the spirit of a figure.[235] In SHUTTER ISLAND, a storm is about to break out when the character, which, in the beginning, goes with the name Teddy (Leonardo di Carpio), arrives at the island. As more this character is in turmoil, the worse the weather get. The storm subsides the moment the protagonist accepts his true identity.

These examples were intended to provide an initial orientation as to how space can be used to convey explicit and above all implicit dramaturgy in contemporary films, even though the possibilities for variation emerging from this fundamental principle are manifold.

Impact of Time

In modern dramaturgy, one can adapt not only space but also time to the narrative. Space and time are inextricably linked. In contrast to the spaciousness, one experiences time as relatively independent of human influence. In physics, time is inherent, unalterable and independent. The concept of time in religion is that time is of divine or eternal characteristic.[236] The Bible gives architecture of the time rather than a geography or topography of events,[237] connecting the concept of eternal with the momentum of an incident embedded in plot and story. It should be noted that within the structure of the Old Testament/Torah, time and events are not told chronologically, but ordered according to their meaning. Hence, for arranging a dramatic narration, different categories of time apply.

Nevertheless, our perception of the passage of time is related to our heartbeat and the experience of a chronology of life. The passage of time

---

235 Pichler & Pollach 2006, p. 450
236 Benjamin 1991a
237 Herschel 1951, pp. 6–10

is experienced and remembered differently depending on the event and circumstances. In the classic drama, time is definite, structured and absolute; in an epic and open narrative, one can shape time sequences, as well as leaps through time and space, according to the plot and theme.[238]

In modern times, the time frame of a dramatic narrative is no longer limited to the course of a day, as the rules of European theatre have recommended since the Renaissance.[239] One can arrange the passage of time differently in a film by applying an epic or open form. Aristotle suggests in the *Poetics* that beginning and end should be arranged in relation to each other. And he adds that the epic way allows narrating several levels of the actions as happening at the same time. Accordingly, different scenes are related to each other. With this form of design, you can entertain the audience as well, because they look at the developing events anew with each scene.[240]

The modern, open dramaturgy evolves from these traditions, a few of which I introduced above. If a modern film narrative built according to priming traditions or even dialectically designed, then a tension curve always emerges. In films, authors/directors and their team can create different experiences of time.[241] Thus the Chronotopos must be carefully constructed to establish a balance between time and space, as already presented in chapter one.

Since a story can be fragmented in modern dramaturgy, time can also be arranged as detached, non-chronological, and moving in various directions. Thus, in modern and postmodern films, the representation of time can be designed according to the approach and theme of the film. Depending on the circumstances and dramaturgical principles introduced and established in the exposition of a movie, each section of the plot can be given its own time and rhythm. So the action no longer has to follow a chronological course of time. The passage of time that provides direction and rhythm to the storyline can even be indefinite. Different dimensions of time can be interconnected. One can arrange the progression of time as running

---

238 Benjamin 1991a; Hegel 2003; Szondi 1987
239 cf. Fiebach 2015, p. 107; Scaliger et al.
240 Aristoteles & Schmitt 2008, chapter 24, b25 - b30
241 Cf. i.a. Becker 2004; Murch 2001

forward and/or backwards, as in ARRIVAL (Villeneuve USA 2016) or DÉJÀ VU (Scott USA 2006). In both movies, some of the characters are shown as experiencing a different flow of time. In ARRIVAL, the humans live in a linear and chronological time, but when they are in the room where they can communicate with the aliens, the time changes its rhythm and direction.

The story can begin in a time before humans emerged on earth and end in the unpredictable future somewhere in the universe, STAR TREK (Roddenberry, USA 1966–1969), 2001 – A SPACE ODYSSEY (Kubrick UK/USA 1968); it can span a lifetime, CITIZEN KANE (Welles USA 1941); or three generations – THE HOURS (Daldry USA/UK 2002), few years, as GAME OF THRONES; a summer – VARGTIMMEN [THE HOUR OF THE WOLF] (Bergman S 1968) or DET SJUNDE INSEGLET [THE SEVENTH SEAL] (Bergman 1957), few weeks - BLACK SWAN (Aronofski USA 2010); or any other time frame the story is situated within - SOLARIS (Tarkovsky USSR 1972), THE MATRIX (Wachowsi&Wachowski, USA 1999), GRAVITY (Cuarón, UK/USA 2013), to name a few examples.

In chronological narrated films, time is often part of the explicit dramaturgy. In an action or science fiction movie, usually something has to be done or achieved within a particular time frame. Snake Plissken (Kurt Russel) has to rescue the president within twenty-four hours in ESCAPE FROM NEW YORK (Carpenter USA 1981); the assassin has to be detected before the celebrations in THE DAY OF THE JACKAL (Zinnemann, UK/F 1973); the rescue weapon must be put together before the comet hits earth in THE FIFTH ELEMENT (Besson, F 1997) to mention a few.

If the places where the different parts of the plot take place are geographically distant, then the explicit dramaturgy can be designed as a chronological lapse of time to give the plot stability, as in NINE LIVES (Garcia USA 2005) or SYRIANA (Gaghan USA 2005). In these two films, time is of great importance for the explicit narrative that connects different places and people. For this reason, the action must be structured chronologically. In both films, an event results from the previous one. Thus, this particular dramaturgical basic rule for causal narration gives these films their stability, conveys a moment of familiarity in the structure despite the fragmentary narrative.

As stated above, it is possible to arrange time flexibly in modern film narrations. It can flow in different directions, jump forwards and backwards, run parallel or stop for a moment. Action sections can have different tempos. This handling of time results from the knowledge of Einstein and other scientists as well as from the quantum theory. To repeat this: In any case, any narrative, regardless of how the passage of time is arranged, requires a well composed Chronotopos. Non-linear narratives pose a significant challenge in this regard.

Leitmotif and Acoustic Counterpoint

This sub-chapter focuses on a few selected aspects of implicit dramaturgy related to audio design. With this, I will give a short introduction to the meaning and the possibilities of the acoustic level within the implicit drama-turgy. It is not possible to cover the entire and complex material of film music and sound design here.

The leitmotif, known from music theory, is a structurally formative element of symphonic works as well as of musical theatre. It is particularly familiar from the works of Richard Wagner. Mostly a leitmotif is composed as a short melody, tone sequence or a specific sound. The instrumentation also gives additional meaning to the leitmotif and underscores the theme of the plot. Accordingly, it evokes an emotional response.

In dramaturgy, the concept of the leitmotif can also be adopted for dra-matic works that do not belong to musical theatre. The leitmotif as a dra-maturgical principle is an artistic sign that represents or supports the theme of the film. It makes it possible to make cross-connections without having to pronounce and explain them. For example, Ibsen used the technique of the dramaturgical leitmotif to make the past appear in the present. The leitmotif design of his works enabled him to relate recent events to contemporary developments. A leitmotif can be a sound – the *Dies Irae* in THE SHINING or *The Hall of the Mountain King*[242] Fritz Lang's M – EINE STADT SUCHT EINEN MÖRDER [M] (Lang D 1931). Ramin Djawadi composed a leitmotif for the GAME OF THRONES series as such, and also leitmotifs for every house and every one of the main characters. A leitmotif can appear as a thought, or/and a phrase – as 'I saw everything in Hiroshima. Everything' in HIROSHIMA MON AMOUR (Resnais, F 1959) or 'Winter is coming' in

---

242 Grieg 1997

GAME OF THRONES as it reflects on 'War is coming' in *Henry VI*[243]. It can also be presented through an artefact – the rifle in BABEL (Iñárritu, F/USA/MEX 2006), a picture, a dress, a colour, a particular view. To establish cross-connections and to recall the theme, a leitmotif can be used several times in a narrative, yet sparingly. If it's used too intrusively and therefore appears like a signpost, it fails its purpose.

Music and sound design are hence a fundamental part of film dramaturgy. They are essential for designing the visual-acoustic counterpoint and the 'aesthetic conflict' and supporting implicit dramaturgy in modern and postmodern movies. 'Hearing is a way of touching at a distance and the intimacy of the first sense is fused with sociability whenever people gather together to hear something special.'[244] Consequently, the technology to distribute movies in cinemas of any kind responds to this fact. Sound and music design add a touching effect to the movie, which is sensually received. 'Hearing and touch meet when the lower frequencies of audible sound pass over tactile vibrations (at about 20 hertz). (...) The sense of hearing cannot be closed off by will. There are no earlids'.[245]

In using sound and music in movies, one can choose from many opportunities. One is to illustrate and support an illusion of reality. 'Music must follow visual incidents and illustrate them either by directly imitating them or by using clichés that are associated with the mood or the content of the picture.'[246] Sound and music design can support the impression of an illusion of reality or emphasise the artistic quality of a movie, whether with the help of a composed soundtrack or by using stock music. Using stock music is one way of giving a movie its acoustic tone. Martin Scorsese and Quentin Tarantino, for example, integrate pre-produced music, pop music as well as concert hall compositions, to amalgamate an additional meaning, in terms of implicit dramaturgy.

Music has the power to link a reference framework to a story and to reveal the inner life of acting characters in a way that cannot be expressed in any other way. In an instant, music can deepen the effect of a scene or

---

243 *Herny VI*, in: Shakespeare 1962, p. 502–595
244 Schafer 1993, position 286
245 Ibid., position 286
246 Eisler 1947, p. 12

bring an aspect of the story into sharper focus. It can have a telling effect on how the characters in the story appear – on how we perceive what they are feeling or thinking – and it can reveal or expand upon subjective aspects and values associated with places and ideas intrinsic to the drama. Further, music being a temporal art, it can have an enormous impact on the pacing of events, moving things along when needed, dwelling on something that requires attention, accenting this or that instant or an event to help to bring out the various connections and divergent point of views.[247]

Adorno and Eisler write about the 'function and dramaturgy' of music for film and refer in particular to the harmonic-contrapuntal element of occidental music[248]. One aspect they discuss is how music can contribute to the production of a motion picture from a dramaturgical point of view. They emphasise that music should not be used ornamentally but as 'an essential addition to the meaning of the scene – this is its dramaturgic justification.'[249] Following this thought, music can be part of the visual-acoustic counterpoint. 'Music, instead of limiting itself to conventional reinforcement of the action or mood, can throw its meaning into relief by setting itself in opposition to what is being shown on the screen.'[250]

Gabriel Yared[251], for example, defines himself as 'a composer for films, not a film composer'[252]. He prefers to be involved from the very first stage of film production and hence develops his music from the story told by the director or from reading the script.[253] This enables him to compose a piece of music, which can stand on its own and serves the film well.

Visual and acoustic design can complement each other to establish an aesthetic/cinematic conflict or to form a dramaturgical equivalent to musical counterpoint. The counterpoint in music gives every voice a meaning, and together they accord a form and theme to an artwork.[254]

---

247 Burt 1994, p. 4
248 Eisler 1947, p. 21
249 Ibid., p. 24
250 Ibid., p. 26
251 Composer for about 118 films, e.g. THE ENGLISH PATIENT (Minghella, USA/ UK 1996)
252 Sweet 2018, 10 min
253 Ibid., 6 min
254 Cf. Adorno 2003, p. 91/92

Music has an impact on film, and film has an impact on music. Whether we are conscious of this, it is through interaction that the full force of their combined effect comes into play. In music, the word *counterpoint* is applied to situations involving two or more lines, where each line has a sense of independence or integrity of its own. When combined, they make a statement that is larger than each of the component parts. In our case, there is no question that because of the fundamental difference between the two media – one is visual, the other aural – each is inevitably perceived as having independence of its own. When placed together, a great deal more is expressed than would be possible by means of either medium alone. Indeed, one will heighten the effect of the other.[255]

To mention another example, Guzmán works with music and sound in terms of the counterpoint in his film THE PEARL BUTTON (Guzmán 2015). José Miguel Miranda, José Miguel Tobar, and Hugues Maréchal composed the music. In Guzmán's documentary, water in all its forms is of centrality. The film starts with the sound of the ocean and pictures of glaciers and rain. Shortly after, as part of the exposition, the anthropologist (Claudio Mercado), who is one of the main characters, got filmed near a stream. In this situation, he reflects on the sound of water, which in the thinking of Native Americans is alive. 'So water is a source of music.'[256] Mercado reflects on the importance of water for planet earth and life in general, to come back to sound and music, its composition and polyphonic character. Then he starts to sing an overtone melody portraying the water as he learned it from the indigenous people. With this situation, at the explicit level of the narration, Guzman establishes the point of convergence and connects the theme, visual storytelling, and sound design. Water is the element that allows Guzman to connect the dialectic of life and death, history and future. Here, water becomes a sign of Chile's cultural memory. This dramaturgical approach makes it possible to break down several levels of the narrative on which he describes the various aspects of the film's multifaceted theme. These include, among other things, the crime committed during Pinochet's dictatorship against the indigenous population, in particular to a tribe that lives on Chile's shores. At all levels and episodes, the question of the significance of memory for the identity of a society remains central.[257]

---

255 Burt 1994, p. 6
256 Guzmán 2015, 7 min
257 Guzman was awarded with the Bear for the category Best Screenplay for this film at the Berlinale Film Festival 2015

Sound design and the choice of music not only support rhythm, pace, and mood within the explicit level of dramaturgy but are equally a vital part of implicit dramaturgy. Sound can also underpin the representation of time and space within the chronotopos.

V-Effekt – The Alienation-Effect

The Alienation-Effect is known from Brecht's theatre practice as well as his theoretical reflections on it.[258] It is a technique derived from tradition. Brecht refers therefore to Victor Hugo, William Shakespeare, James Joyce, Johann Wolfgang von Goethe, and other authors who practised such an effect in their works before him.[259] Brecht emphasises the importance to focus on the changeability of conditions and hence the changeability of a human being. *Man Equals Man*[260] by Brecht, premiered 1926 in Berlin, is mentioned here as one notable example. Following his approach, to emphasise its central features, a writer/director has to show the materialist-sensual world in a poetic intensification. To achieve this in the performative practice, some abstraction is needed to describe and perform events as they happen as precisely and sensuously as possible. The method of acting should be made transparent to give the audience a signal that the actors are representing characters not imitating them. An active audience consequently becomes a productive recipient who will compare the performance with their experience and knowledge.[261] Brecht aimed to invite the audience to think about events performed for them – which is, for example, very similar to Dziga Vertov's argumentation in his manifesto 'Cine-Eye', published 1924.[262] The audience thus might be inspired to reflect on how they would act in a similar situation.

Movies applying a technique congeneric to Brecht's Alienation Effect are amongst others BLACK SWAN (Aronofski, USA 2010), in which the main character is shown as metamorphosing into different forms of appearance (Fig. 36), THE SHINING with Jack Nicholson demonstrating

---

258 Brecht 1966a, pp. 99–101
259 Brecht 1967, pp. 362–365
260 Brecht 1979
261 Cf. i.a. Burdorf Fasbender, Moennighoff, et al. 2007; Hecht 1979, pp. 102–106; Rancière 2011
262 Vertov 1984

the character of Jack (Fig. 37), and THE PIRATES OF THE CARIBBEAN (Verbinski USA 2003) with Jonny Depp interpreting Jack Sparrow (Fig. 38). In all of these movies, a chosen gestus[263] is established in dialectic correspondence to the situation the character is confronted with. This approach emphasises the typicality of a particular character. This performative act also establishes an ironic distance. Clearly, in demonstrating a character, the actor/actress has to keep the figure believable within the aesthetic style of the work.

Fig. 36: BLACK SWAN   Fig. 37: THE SHINING   Fig. 38: THE PIRATES
OF THE CARIBBEAN

In a particular moment within the overall performance or movie, a character can abandon his role for a moment, stepping out of the action and comment on it, although they are still that character but reflecting on the situation. Consequently, they can speak directly to the audience or to themselves. For example, the main character of HOUSE OF CARDS, no matter which production we are reflecting on, addresses the audience directly. So does Francis Urquhart (Ian Richardson) in the original BBC series from 1990 (Seed UK 1990), and Francis Underwood (Kevin Spacey) in the first six seasons of the Netflix-Adaptation (USA, 2013-). Other examples are STARS (Wolf, GDR 1959) as most of the films by Konrad Wolf, JADUP AND BOEL (SIMON, GDR 1980) and EUROPE, EUROPE (Holland, D/F/PL 1990) next others mentioned already above in the sub-chapter on inversion and framing.

---

263 Brecht 1966a, pp. 73–77; 1966f, p. 223

Thus, the 'fourth wall'[264] cracks, and the audience involved. The spectators are invited to behave towards the plot; as an audience understood as at eye level. The alienation effect is not limited to the acting, although in the theatre acting is particularly central in achieving this effect. In films, the alienation effect can also be achieved through the overall aesthetic design, camera management, editing, and sound design. In some works, the commentary comes out of the off. All in all, this approach should convey a fascinating, touching and entertaining performance.

'The Unreliable Narration' and Irony

That term *unreliable narrator* emerges from literature studies. It primarily reflects on a particular artifice in literary storytelling. An unreliable narrator is introduced already in works such as *A True Story* by Lucian of Samosata[265] and *The Golden Ass* by Apuleius[266]. Although the principle of the unreliable narrator exists throughout the history of literature, a distinction between reliable and unreliable is made for the first time in 1961 by Wyne C. Both: 'I have called a narrator *reliable* when he speaks for or acts in accordance with the norms of the work (which is so to say, the implied author's norms), *unreliable* when he does not.'[267]

Often the unreliable narrator is presented as a manifestation of irony. With the means of irony, the mediation of information can be split up. The unreliable narrator delivers explicit and implicit messages that are contradictory. The implicit message contrasts with the explicit narrative level.[268] The resulting irritating moments and surprising twists contribute to the entertainment and suspense. They support the artistic effect. This narrative attitude represents the principle of the omniscient narrator.

As a medium and consequently, when it comes to reception, film and literature are quite different. While reading one can stop, take a break, and

---

264 'Fourth wall' is a traditional term describing the imagined wall between stage and audience, often used for films as well, and understanding the screen as fourth wall.
265 Samosata, p. 180
266 *Metamorphoseon libri XI [The Golden Ass]*, 2. cent.
267 Booth 1983, p. 158/159
268 Cf. Martínez & Scheffel 2007, pp. 100–104

turn back a few pages, etcetera. While watching a narrative-performative work, one follows the events unfolding as if experiencing it as an eyewitness.[269] Very seldom does one stop a film on first viewing or rewind it. It's impossible to interrupt a show or performance when you're in the theatre or cinema. Against this background, the concept of an 'unreliable narrator', as it is established within literary studies, must be modified for film dramaturgy due to the specifics of an audio-visual narrative work. And since it is also a descriptive term with an interpretative character, it is not easy to adapt it for film dramaturgy. As already mentioned, dramaturgy reflects the process of film production. An analytical understanding of the artisitic practice strives for or supports an adequate aesthetic design. In dramaturgy, terms are predominantly analytical and dialectical.

Since every narrator in a film is part of the work, the aspect of the unreliable must be made one of the traits of this character, as for example for the character with the name Verbal (Kevin Spacey) who is at the same time the role Keyser in THE USUAL SUSPECTS (Singer, USA/G 1995).

In order to achieve an 'unreliable narration', a film must be very well constructed explicitly and implicitly. One can obtain an aesthetic equivalent of unreliability as one form of postmodern aesthetics within the dramaturgy of an open form.[270] An impression of unreliability can come about when the explicit level is designed in such a way that the audience permanently concentrates on the coherent evolving plot. Therefore, one can use traditions of cinematic narrative as well as genre conventions. In the course of the plot, however, aesthetic signals repeatedly point out that there may be different levels of story. The 'unreliable narrator' results from a cleverly designed dramaturgical play with the audience. Such a game with conventions is part of the plot building in USUAL SUSPECTS. What is to be emphasised here is that the protagonist, Verbal/Keyser Soze (Kevin Spacey), acts as an unreliable narrator for all other characters within the plot, but not for the audience. Nevertheless, since that this is written and directed to be so, some viewers feel deceived, as they go along with the central figure and perceive the course of the plot from his perspective. But if you watch the film carefully and not just emotionally immersed, you can see that the

269 Cf. Lotman 1977
270 Cf. Stutterheim and Lang 2013

person who goes with the name Verbal, when addressing the audience directly, conveys information that leaps through time and space. His off texts are reliable although they are intertwined with dialogues directed to other roles, which are not. The fact that the character is not what the other characters think he would also be reflected in conventions of a thriller genre. The effect of 'unreliable narration' in this film results from the dramaturgical design of the entire movie. The figure with the name Dean Keaton (Gabriel Byrne) is the one that invites to empathy or at least sympathy. The dramaturgical significance of the figure is emphasised by the fact that this figure is in the centre of the action of the first sequence of the film. This situation anticipates the fate of this figure. As already mentioned above, this situation is an inversion. An inversion is a dramaturgical principle with which an event from the later course of the action is placed in front of it. The interest of the audience is directed by this form of design. In this film, this dramaturgical form makes it possible to lead the tension to the increasingly urgent question of who Keyser Soze is? Likewise, the figure of Keaton is at the centre of the dramatic plot. This construction also corresponds to the genre-typical hero, who is not represented by 'Verbal', who appears passive or even helpless over long passages. Playing with genre conventions is part of the dramaturgical concept here, which results in an, for most viewers, unexpected ending to the story that but is logical and believable. The character Keyser Soze is a schemer, conveying contradictory messages. Thus this film comes as close as possible to the concept of an 'unreliable narrator', according to the possibilities of the medium. As in literature, the principle of an – customised – unreliable narrator can give this expectation ironic refraction. To establish a level of reference, which plays with conventions is a dramaturgical strategy to enrich the texture of the story and simultaneously to attain an alienation effect by creating distance. In a situation of ironic communication, the narrator delivers the explicit and implied message at the same time.[271] Hence, the challenge for writing and directing such work is demanding, and one should not underestimate it.

---

271 Martínez and Scheffel 2007, p. 100

Analytic, Episodic, Epic, Ensemble, and Multi-Perspective Movies

In the course of film history, dramaturgical models evolve with the Zeitgeist, historical events and artistic movements. This chapter will give an overview of and introduction to selected models and their application. From a dramaturgical perspective, the selection reflects on most frequently used models in film and TV productions. Dramaturgy knows of more options, but those introduced here are the most relevant.

The Well-Made-Movie and its Analytical Structure

Many movies use the dramaturgy of *well-made play* and the principles of an analytical drama, which are traditionally related to each other. The *well-made play* emerged in the middle of the 19th century in France, signalling the beginning of the realistic theatre, responding to historical and social changes before and resulting from the revolutions of 1789 and 1846.[272] Influential authors are Eugene Scribe (1791–1861), Alexandre Dumas jun. (1824–1895), Victorian Sardou (1831–1906), and Emile Augier (1820–1889). Their plays represented critical reflections on the state of their society. Soon after, Henrik Ibsen (1828–1906)[273] and August Strindberg (1849–1912) adapted that at that time new dramaturgical approach. Scribe and his fellow writers became known for intrigue-comedies and their "dramaturgy of surprise."[274] Augier, in particular, used irony as an aesthetic tool to contrast miserabe situations in portraits.[275] The well-made play is one of the traditions, which was early on adapted for film productions.[276]

Within an analytical drama, the conflict is initiated by a situation around a secret. Such a secret can be of medical, personal, or public nature. It can be materialised in knowledge by a witness or companion,

---

272 Kindermann 1965, pp. 20–29
273 Biener 1990
274 Kindermann 1965, p. 21
275 Ibid., 1965, p. 35
276 Bordwell et al. 2006

a document or an asset. The main character either has to keep the secret hidden or to discover it, on any account. The opposite party/character is either threatening to make the secret public, use it against the main character to destroy his/her hopes, dreams, social or political striving; or has to keep their secret hidden. Often those conflicting interests form an intrigue/counter-intrigue situation equivalent to the concept of protagonist/antagonist, although in a different configuration and rules. The main character is accordingly a "modern character" as introduced above. In the films known to me, which follow this dramaturgical tradition, the main characters are not involved in the original event the secret is about, but accidentally connected to what it contains. Therefore, that principle is the blueprint for crime stories, detective stories, and thrillers. In the end, one does not have to reveal the mystery entirely. It can be left with the audience to think about the solution as a conclusion derived from the action, information, and signs, which were part of the narration – as in *Rosmersholm* by Henrik Ibsen[277] as well as THE USUAL SUSPECTS (Singer, USA/G 1995) and INSIDE MAN (S. Lee, USA 2006), for example. The technique of a "well-made movie" is first to tell an array of events in a fast tempo. Secondly, within these sequences, situations are composed in which one character may be ready to reveal or discern the secret, the hidden cause, or just an element to get closer. In the very last moment, something happens. A phone rings or someone knocks at the door or enters the scene hence postponing the revelation. To make these situations convincing and to give the audience not too much time to think about what might have been revealed, one needs a fast pace.[278]

The dramaturgical principle of intrigue and counter-intrigue is related to the concept of the well-made play and analytical drama. These patterns that are established within film dramaturgy mostly serve the thriller genre and most of the detective-stories but also the melodrama. Most famous in this regard might be *The Talented Mr Ripley* by Patricia Highsmith.[279]

---

277 Ibsen 1927; Szondi 1965, pp. 30/31; Szondi 1987, p. 17
278 Cf. Kindermann 1965, p. 22
279 Highsmith 1957

Intrigue and Counter-Intrigue — THE DAY OF THE JACKAL

An excellent example to explain and understand the principles of the intrigue, which is central for analytical dramaturgy, is THE DAY OF THE JACKAL (Zinnemann, UK/F 1973). The action of this movie starts with an incident caused by historical events. A group of people plan the assassination to the president of France at that time, Charles De Gaulle. The assassin fails, the men involved in this assault are arrested and the leader executed. This backstory is shown as the prelude. The prelude, as introduced above, can be a short sequence, which informs about context or an event equivalent to a backstory, and is situated before the exposition. The characters or situation of the prelude don't necessarily have to be part of a linear-causal chronological storyline of the movie, but introduce the plot.

In general, an intrigue arises from an emergency or a vision, reshaping and transforming the personal conflict of a classical drama. With an establishing plan-scene[280], which is a scene in which the intrigant originates a plan, the dramatic action involving an intrigue begins. Such a plan causes a confrontation, which is equivalent to the moment of establishing the conflict in the dramatic narration of the 'closed form'[281]. The schemer incarnates the intrigue. He embodies the interests of a defined social or political group. To accomplish the conspiracy, the schemer needs to disguise, to utilise schemer instruments and a schemer's voice.[282]

The intrigue model as such is understood to be a modern and secular version of conflict construction. In tragedy and accordingly in a movie it is considered to be of a closed-form and thus related to divine destiny, guilt and atonement. In an intrigue construction, the schemer should always should be created as a person convinced of their superiority. The main characteristic of the character of a schemer is that he steadfastly believes that everything achieved results from his actions as well as his unique abilities.

---

280 The term plan-scene in an intrigue construction is established within theatre dramaturgy since the 19th century and defines the scene the plan to start an intrigue is established. Not to be confused with the term often used within an editing context, in which the plan sequence is used for a very long shot without edits showing a particular sequence of the action.

281 Cf. Stutterheim 2015, pp. 126–132

282 Cf. Matt 2006

In a modern intrigue, neither higher power nor fate is involved in the course of events. The intrigant, as designed by the author, triggers the action and determines its development over a specific timeframe.[283] In this movie, the figure going with the nickname 'Jackal' is a prototype for a modern intrigant, as is 'the talented Mr Ripley'.

In THE DAY OF THE JACKAL, the story begins with the group of leaders of the French military underground organisation OAS[284] planning a new attempt to murder Charles De Gaulle. This plan-scene is arranged to run over two situations. The first part shows a meeting of the leaders of the OAS. After the failed assault on De Gaulle, they are desperately looking for another chance to liquidate the president. To make sure that the next, seventh, attempt will be successful, they plan to hire a professional assassin (as introduced already on page 45). This situation, which in dramaturgical terms is defined as 'plan-scene'[285], establishes the primary dramaturgical thread. Resulting from that plan-scene the action leads to the assassination attempt and hence, the moment of the 'catastrophe' in the fifth act. In this movie, the promising British candidate, who goes with the cover name 'Jackal' (Edward Fox), was invited to a kind of job interview and agreed to be the man. Thus, he becomes established as the figure of a schemer. Since this character is representing a principle, a concept, he has consequently no name in this movie. Historical circumstances make the story of THE DAY OF THE JACKAL plausible; the historical context also enriches the aspects of suspense and surprise. This plan-scene weaves in situations that reflect the particular cultural characteristics of the environment in which the characters act or are shaped by. It allows for probable and believable moments of irony to be arranged over two situations.

---

283 Cf. Matt 2006, p. 197

284 Organisation Armée Secrete [Secret Army Organisation] was a short-lived right-wing French paramilitary organization, which carried out terrorist attacks, including bombings and assassinations, in an attempt to prevent Algeria's independence from French colonial rule. Their motto was: "Algeria is French and will remain so." Cf. Harrison 1989

285 Matt 2006, pp. 38–45

The first part of the plan-scene is embedded in the job interview situation when the schemer accepts the order and suggests to the OAS men how they will be able to finance his fee.

The second part of the plan-scene happens when the Jackal entertains his plan to fulfil the task, the assassination. The mission of the schemer is to develop a detailed plan – 'When, where, how'. To allow this plan to become a successful action, the schemer has to prepare material enabling him to become successful. In Zinnemann's movie, this is the main action of act two and hence is a preparation for act four and five. The Jackal designs and orders his instrument – a modified rifle, which he is going to hide in crutches. As part of the disguise, he needs false passports, hair colour, and some drug to change his voice.

At the end of the first act, the counter intrigue and their leading characters are introduced. With our example, they are the minister (Alan Badel) and the commissar Claude Lebel (Michel Lonsdale). Over the first part of the movie, the schemer is the character striving the action, and the commissar reacts to this. Anagnorisis and peripeteia are in this movie situated close to each other and verbally as well as visually emphasised. The moment of anagnorisis happens during the phone call in which the Jackal learns that the police knows about him, his plan in general, and hence that the police is searching for him. In the moment of peripeteia, as the moment of reversal, the conflict the character is facing is visualised. He has to decide whether to continue and thus to risk his life or to stop here and cancel this mission.

Fig. 39: Peripeteia – THE DAY OF THE JACKAL

With this moment, the power to influence the action swaps from one character to the other. From a dramaturgical point of view, from now on the commissar is actively leading the action and the Jackal reacting to it. With an analytical approach, one understands that the steps, which are taken by the commissar, provoke the responses of the Jackal. Now, the figure of the Jackal is shown as reactive. Consequently, the Jackal has to make use of the intrigue-instruments he supplied himself with during act two. These tools will allow him to hide behind other identities. This way, he can proceed with his intrigue throughout act four and the beginning of act five. Augmented by a variant of the schemer's voice fitting for this story, one can believe that this character can make it to the place he intended to use for the planned assassination resulting from his preparations in act two. In act five, in a situation equivalent to catastrophe and catharsis, the commissar detects and overpowers the Jackal. Thus, he prevents the assault in the very last moment. In this scene of their first and only face-to-face confrontation, the intrigue is successfully eliminated. To break down the conspiracy and its schemer also is a feature of this dramaturgical model. This principle reflects on the dramaturgical model of the tragedy. Since Ancient Drama, it is a tradition that the conclusion of a story gives hope for the future of the community, the society, and the social group in the narration.

The composition of the final sequence of every movie is essential for creating a balance within its structure. In THE DAY OF THE JACKAL, as a response to the introduction, in which the professional killer was introduced but his identity not revealed, the last scene shows that the police tries to investigate who the assassin was, but fail.

A more contemporary version applying the intrigue-model is THE GHOST WRITER (Polański UK/F/D 2010). The incident to start the narration is the plan to publish the 'autobiography' of a former premier minister of the United Kingdom, who was involved in historical events – like the Iraq War. An analogy to Tony Blair is apparent. The author who was initially appointed to act as ghost writer died in a presumed accident and must be replaced. In this movie, the plot starts with the unexpected death of the ghost writer, which is the element of the analytical drama used to begin the explicit narration. Events are developing fast, including twists and ellipsis. Thus, as part of the plan-scene, a new ghostwriter has to be appointed. This author should be interested in nothing else other than writing. Therefore, one of the first situations shows the agent having lunch with his author. Shortly afterwards they meet the publisher in his office. Here, the author is interviewed and consequently appointed. So the main character (Ewan McGregor) consistently bears the nickname 'Ghost' and is never addressed by name, just like the Jackal in Zinnemann's film. That character is designed as a 'central self', as explained earlier in this book. Hence, by representing a principle, the figure is as well an embodiment of the uninformed public confronted with a political game. Besides that, the model of an analytic drama and hence the thriller genre is applied here. This movie is arranged chronologically and as a single intrigue-counter-intrigue construction. The two opening scenes within the exposition establish him as the leader of the counter-intrigue, who is as well the positive protagonist.

After he is appointed, the new ghostwriter recieves a manuscript in a bag handed over to him. On the way back from the publishing house, someone attacks the author and steals it. This yellow plastic bag is a 'Red Herring' but designed to direct our attention towards the manuscript and the dangerous situation the ghostwriter will have to face. When the figure of the ghostwriter is waiting at the airport on his way to his new job, he learns - as does the audience - that there will be an investigation into the politician whose autobiography he is supposed to finish. Shortly after his arrival at the estate, it becomes evident that secret background information is hidden in the manuscript. The intrigue is led by two active characters representing a group pursuing a distinct political-economical interest. McGregor's character finds himself confronted with a conspiracy he never expected when hired as the new ghostwriter. The audience is invited to discover the complex background of the story through this main character. Here the technique is used in which the audience knows only as much as the figure acting as the central self. Although Polański does not yet introduce who is representing the intrigue, the dramaturgical patterns applied here are familiar in principle. By shaping the character of the ghostwriter as a central self, this ghostwriter can, as explained above, observe and question events. The film narration lets us, the audience, note how the ghostwriter discovers the circumstances piece by piece. In the moment of anagnorisis, the Ghost finds an envelope with photographs and a phone number, which were assembled by his predecessor. This situation of the peripeteia happens shortly after, when the Ghost uses the car of his predecessor for the first time, and the navigation system suggests an address not familiar to him. After a moment of hesitation, he decides to follow the pre-set navigation. The GPS leads him to one of the people known to him from the file. From this moment on, he is confronted with the initiators of the intrigue. This group tries to prevent the conspiracy from being uncovered at all costs. With the reversal of the plot, the previously uninvolved observer, who reacted in the first half of the film, becomes an actively behaving character. The quality of this film results from the design of the interaction of the characters within the plot, which is supported by the visual dramaturgy. Thus the visual design contributes to the course of the story and its arc of tension just as much as the spoken dialogues.

Fig. 40: THE GHOST WRITER   Fig. 41: THE GHOST WRITER

The aesthetic quality adds implied meaning to the story told. Framing the former premier minister in a position, as shown in figure 40, serves implicit dramaturgy. How he is pictured here reminds of a gesture of a crucified man. The bust in the bookshelf references wars of Ancient times or Ancient Drama, or both. This bookshelf as such is not just part of the home of a publisher but signalises at the same time the world of literature and complexity. The landscape and the weather in the background of the figure tell of a cold and unpleasant atmosphere. When we look at figure 41, the still shows the Ghostwriter alone in front of steel fridges. Cold steel, closed doors. He is alone in the house or at least in that kitchen, where a typical English lunch waits for him. This shot is framed and arranged in a way that shows us that he is cornered in. He hasn't much space for movement. And he is on his own. Throughout this movie, Polański and his director of photography, Pawel Edelmann, as well as the artistic team involved in the production, adds implicit meaning by giving the mise-en-scène a metaphoric implication. Director and cinematographer framed the shots in a way that the background comments on the state of mind of the characters or the overall situation. Ending the movie with the death of the ghostwriter and the manuscript gone with the wind, the schemer stays undiscovered. Thus, this movie breaks with tradition of proposing a better, utopian world.

The principles presented above can be used flexibly and combined with genre conventions to develop a dramaturgical concept that serves the subject and the story to be told. In this way, you can create stories that surprise and fascinate equally, as the above examples already show. Luis Malle, to mention another example, twisted the intrigue-concept in his movie AU REVOIR LES ENFANTS (Malle, F/D/I 1987).[286] When the historical or societal context is of high importance for the implicit dramaturgy and/or the overall story, this can be used to enrich the construction of the intrigue-dramaturgy. Hence characters represent different aspects of such a constellation and accordingly always serve the action. It is perfectly possible to connect two or more intrigue-counter-intrigue constellations in one plot.

For INSIDE MAN (Lee USA 2006) for example, Spike Lee and writer Gurwitz draw too on this tradition. They apply for their movie not just a more complex and expanding intrigue-construction but also the principle of inversion. They dissolve the chronology of time, which usually gives suspense to an action movie. To explain this further would need a more sophisticated analysis in the context of specifications of film dramaturgy in postmodern films than is possible to perform here and now.

Epic Movies as Extended Drama

Epic storytelling, as well as episodic narratives, has been known for a long time, not only from the Bible, the *Mahābhārata*, or the *Rāmāyaṇa*, the *Sampo*, or other epic sagas. The Bible may be the best-known epic work in the Western World. Its texts are situational and biographical, which are told as episodes woven into each other[287]. In literature, the episodic structure of epic narratives is hence familiar. It became part of secular/ fictional storytelling with the invention of the novel and serialised novels

---

286 Stutterheim & Kaiser 2011, p. 17 et seq.; pp. 143–155
287 Cf. Alter 2011; Liss, Bœckler, & Landthaler 2011, p. 6 et seq.

published in newspapers or journals.[288] Epic narratives are attractive to an audience since they give an impression of or become a companion for a chapter in one's life. Apart from this, the epic narration is well known and hence familiar in many parts of the world. Epic movies were and still are produced in all parts of the world since the beginning of film history. Amongst others: INTOLERANCE (D. W. Griffith, USA 1916), BIRTH OF A NATION (D.W. Griffith, USA 1915), Иван Грозный [IVAN THE TERRIBLE] (Eisenstein, USSR 1944/58), BEN HUR (Wyler, USA 1959), ELISABETH (Kapur, UK 1998), HIROSHIMA MON AMOUR (Resnais, F 1959), NOSTALGIA (Tarkovsky, I/USSR 1983), Out of Africa (Pollack, USA/UK 1985), THE ENGLISH PATIENT (Minghella, USA/UK 1996), THE MAHABHARATA (Brook 1990), 刺客聶隱娘 [THE ASSASSIN] (Huo, TWN/CHN/HKG 2015).

One should not confuse the dramaturgical term epic with the use of the word in the everyday language, where it describes something which takes very long or is tedious. An epic narration is not characterised by stretching an event into long sequences but by telling about events, which may span an extended timeframe and could include a journey through vast territories. From the very beginning, the attribution epic consists of the reflection on historical circumstances or/and Zeitgeist of that period. Hegel describes epic narration as a medium to reflect on the world in its totality by representing it through art.[289] In this context, the term totality emphasises that the approach to telling a particular story is not just to narrate the single individual fate but rather the relationship of a person to the historical reality in all its complexity. This outlook includes portraying power structures the characters is confronted with. Hence, in an epic movie, such circumstances as the historical moment, a social movement, and/or a political change translate into a personal faith, which is representing the "collective level". This aspect includes religious beliefs, the concrete entity, political and domestic life, as well as the livelihood and enjoyments of human existence.[290] The individual level is personifying the collective layer of the plot. An epic tells about the relation of the individual to the entity of the cosmos from which the story unfolds. One can reflect on the historical,

---

288 Fiedler 2017, p. 25 et seq.
289 Hegel 2003, pp. 106–108
290 Ibid., pp. 115–118

social, cultural state of society through content that can and should be part of the epic narration. And, importantly, an epic narrative-performative work always reflects on or demonstrates its artificiality. 'The deconstruction of illusion in the modern 'drama' (...), leads to that aestheticised representation of reality supplied by all epic writing.'[291]

Brecht developed his concept about the Epic Theatre out of this philosophical-aesthetic tradition.[292] He also emphasises the individual artistic approach of epic performative art. Epic movies are in this sense as poetic as the epic theatre was and still is. These artistic-narrative performances represent the creative transformation of the world we live in.

> An artistic discovery occurs each time as a new and unique image of the world, a hieroglyphic of absolute truth. It appears at a revelation, as a momentary, absolute wish to grasp intuitively and at a stroke all the laws of this world—its beauty and ugliness, its compassion and cruelty, its infinity and its limitations. The artist expresses these things by creating the image, sui generis detector of the absolute. Through the image is sustained an awareness of the infinite: the eternal within the finite, the spiritual within matter, the limitless given form.[293]

Since all these texts and traditions, as mentioned above and elsewhere, are part of the Cultural Memory[294], film dramaturgy is echoing these traditions of epic narration. Features which are significant within epic storytelling, are essential for modern film dramaturgy too.

An epic tells either about a historical event, a life or a significant event in the lifetime of a person or for a social group. Therefore, one can stretch the period it takes for the chain of events to unfold. It can be stretched over months, years or centuries and concentrated at one place, spread over a country, a continent or throughout the universe in all its dimensions. Neither time nor space have to be directed, arranged chronologically or be consistent. The narrated time can change its pace, can slow down, stop or jump. It can become elliptic or circular.

An epic movie implies open, modern dramaturgy. Hence one can tell a story about a situation primed by an actual condition. Such an approach

---

291 Szondi 1987, p. 84
292 Brecht, 1948; Benjamin 1977; Brecht 1966d; Brecht 1966c
293 Tarkovsky 1986, p. 37
294 A. Assmann 2011; J. Assmann 2004, 2011

can be represented by one or more individual characters either in a real-istic, or mythological or legendary, fantastic genre convention. The visual narration is part of the storytelling, and one also can design landscapes as character-like appearances, as in CAST AWAY (Zemeckis USA 2000). Emotions and thoughts are shown, visualised, and evoked through audio-visual aesthetics, not just described or expressed in dialogues. The development of these processes can be caused by circumstances, an incident, a dream or hope.

The Technique of Presenting the Epic Self as the Modern Protagonist

The epic protagonist can be designed and impersonated in various ways. According to the features introduced above, these main characters reflect on a 'total individual'.[295] He or she can be of a complacent, a shy or hesitant nature, or just a flâneur. The essence of an epic protagonist is the artistic representation of an individual presented as part of a socio-historical world.

Thornton Wilder's *Our Town* (1938) is is sometimes looked upon as the work of an author who established the epic protagonist in the modern theatre of the 20th century[296], although Bertolt Brecht already applied this technique in his plays. Wilder introduces the character likened to a stage manager who 'stood outside the thematic space in the pivotal position occupied by the narrator.' This stage manager is shown as 'conscious of the roles of the roles and thus, represents a subject-object relationship external to them – precisely that epic relationship existing between the narrator and his object.'[297] His character is actor and observer at once.

> 'Therefore, he (Wilder) had to give his heroes at least the beginnings of a dramatic life, despite the fact that this life did not unfold in the sphere of conflict and decision. Uniform, uneventful, deeply impersonal, and tedious events became immediate/interpersonal events and require the appearance of uniqueness.'[298]

---

295 Hegel 2003, p. 300
296 Szondi 1987, p. 84
297 Ibid., p. 84
298 Ibid., p. 83

This character, as an epic self, addresses the audience directly by commenting on the events or adding information and thoughts. This character metaphorically reflects on the life and emotional state of its time.

Epic characters represent aspects of their time. Notwithstanding the above requirements, one can design them as appropriate beauteous human characters. Their acts should echo the main events, the theme and situation, of the epic narration. The single individual figure is not purely acting as him or herself but as one representing the embodiment of the experience of a group of people. The circumstances cause distinctive acting.[299]

Carrière writes about danger of the epic narrative consisting of the fact that one can be tempted by the most simple figures to a draw in black-and-white. Great authors, however, give voice to emotions and inner worlds of thought regardless of how their characters have to live through it.[300] Therefore, epic films will often deal with events in which the main character(s) either do their utmost to fulfil their hopes but repeatedly encounter obstacles to their endeavours. CHILDREN OF THE PARADISE (Carné, F 1945) or EARTH (Mehta IND 1998) by Deepa Mehta can be mentioned here as examples. Mehta tells about the dreams, hopes, desires, and hate of a group of people around the center figure Lenny (Maia Sethna). Each of these characters who are accompanying Lenny represent exemplarily a different ethnic, religious or social group at that time of historical change.

Triggered by a traumatic situation, the character of BARRY LYNDON (UK/USA Kubrick 1975) develops his desire to become equally rich and feared. His story represents a metaphor. And Lyndon resembles Tarkovsky's Ivan. Both represent a character 'that had been destroyed, shifted of his axis'[301]. Due to traumatic events, something 'had gone irretrievably out of his life. And the thing he had acquired, like an evil gift from the war, in place of what has been his own, was concentrated and heightened within him.'[302]

---

299 Hegel 2003, pp. 145–148
300 Carrièr 1999, p. 221
301 Tarkovsky 1986, p. 17
302 Ibid., p. 17

An epic protagonist acts and reflects on his action. They are involved and distanced at the same time, participate within the action and address the audience.[303]

Episodic Narration

An episodic narrative represents a particular form of organising a story in which the plot can be broken down into fragments that contain seemingly independent sequences. Each episode includes a short continuous scene. Episodes shouldn't fall apart incoherently. One must design them in such a way that the overall narrative progresses, and the central theme develops. Hence, all these episodes must be connected thematically. The method of organising the material as episodes into an intricate work has a long tradition. Its beginning lies in the Ancient Theatre,[304] this principle can be found in *One Thousand and One Nights*[305] as well as in the composition of the epistolary novel, as for example *Clarissa* by Samuel Richardson (1748), *Geschichte des Fraueleins von Sternberg [History of the damsel von Sternberg]* by Sophie von La Roche (1771) or *Les liaisons dangereuses [Dangerous Liaisons]* by Choderlos de Laclos (1782), to mention a few. Episodes are as well the term for the parts of series, no matter if a serialised novel is published in a newspaper or produced as a TV- or web-series.

The following sub-chapter presents some of the relevant traditions from which the dramaturgy of the episodic narrative in the modern film derives. Films that tell biographical or historical stories, but also road movies, documentaries and of course series can be arranged episodically. Episodic narratives can be linked at the explicit level by places, leitmotifs, one or more objects – as the banknote in DIE ABENTEUER EINES ZEHNMARKSCHEINES [ADVENTURES OF A TEN MARK NOTE] (Viertel, D/USA 1926), the rifle in BABEL (Iñárritu, F/USA/MEX 2006), the bomb in SYRIANA (Gaghan, 2005); or the topographic place the action is situated within – as in 羅生門 RASHŌMON (KUROSAWA, J 1950), NINE LIVES (Garcia, USA

303 Cf. Stutterheim 2015, pp. 294–300
304 Träger 1986, p. 137
305 Burton 1985

2005), or A PRAIRIE HOME COMPANION: THE LAST RADIO SHOW (Altman USA 2006) and MENSCHEN AM SONNTAG [People on Sunday] (Siodmak, Ulmer, Gliese, Siodmak, & Zinnemann, D 1930); or by a theme – Նռան գույնը [THE COLOR OF POMEGRANATES] (Parajanov, USSR 1969), AZ ÉN XX. SZÁZADOM [MY TWENTIETH CENTURY] (Enyedi, H/D/CUB 1989) or 夢 [Dreams] (Kurosawa, J 1990).

The theme represented in the essential meaning and the point of convergence aligns all episodes. The central theme is always determined by the attitude and approach of of the particular author who wrote it and hence modified in every episode. Such compositions can be supported by audio-visual levels of dramaturgy.

One of the most discussed episodic films may well be COFFEE AND CIGARETTES (Jarmusch USA 2003) by Jim Jarmusch. It is Jarmusch's third episodic movie, this time a compilation of different short films of which the first were initially produced independently as short films. These two shorts initiated the production of COFFEE AND CIGARETTES as a feature-length movie.[306] Jarmusch applies some aesthetic principles to all episodes, which give the overall film a texture.[307] The top shot of the particular table connects all episodes.

Moreover, it is the theme which connects and develops throughout all episodes. All characters are talking about relationships – amongst family, friends or that between private and public. That is expressed through the motif of resonance. Every episode has its song or sound. Jarmusch culminates the point of convergence and hence its central theme in Alfred Molinas 'All I want, I don't want anything, is to acknowledge this ordinary thing, and, just – love me' in the episode 'Cousins'. Dramaturgically, the arrangement of episodes in COFFEE AND CIGARETTES resembles the basic dramaturgy for a dramatic narration. Jarmusch calls it 'a feature disguised as shorts.'[308]

NINE LIVES (Garcia, USA 2005) is a movie which spans nine episodes. Each of these episodes tells about an unexpected situation in the life of

306 Maurer & Jarmusch 2006, p. 290
307 Raskin 2002, pp. 46–49
308 Abeel 2014

a woman, which influence her life and most likely that of others. Several events are happening, which next day are remembered with amusement or regret by the character(s) involved. These situations take place at different times and distant locations. They seem only accidentally connected. With a closer look, the events or actions happening in these single episodes are dramaturgically interconnected. On the explicit level of the story elements, all episodes refer to communication within relationships and families, most to motherhood. Implicit here is the hint to think "about a child's concept of time. It is interesting stuff, you know."[309]

The effect of these episodes within the overall plot evolves from seemingly random events in the lives of the various characters who seem to meet each other by chance. The texture gives an impression of the cosmos of an exemplary city in the USA.[310]

STILL LIFE - THE GOOD PEOPLE OF THE THREE GORGES

The original Chinese title is a direct reference to *Der gute Mensch von Sezuan* [*The Good Woman Of Setzuan*] by Brecht/Berlau/Steffin (1938–1940), translated as '*The Good People of The Three Gorges*'. The story of Zhangke's movie is situated in the province of Setzuan, in Fengjie, where the Three Gorges dam is about to be built.

The main character the movie introduces first, going with the name Sanming (Han Sanming). He travels from another province, Shanxi, to the city Fengjie. He is searching for his daughter, who disappeared with his wife, who left him dreaming of a better life in that city. In the middle part a woman, Shen Hong (Zhao Tao), from the very same province, is searching for her husband, who went to Fengjie for a job. The switched protagonist in the middle of the film mirrors the character of the first chapter from a different perspective. In the third part, the character Sanming the movie began with, has learned from both episodes.

---

309 Garcia USA 2005, min 19
310 Cf. Stutterheim 2015, p. 305

Fig. 42: STILL LIFE   Fig. 43: STILL LIFE

The male character is a mineworker (Fig. 42) who represents traditional China, whereas the female character the modern. He hopes to reunify his family. She came to ask her husband for a divorce. Both characters and their motifs represent the impact politic can have onto a life of ordinary people. By having a mirrored part showing a different course and outcome, Zhangke may respond here to the dramaturgical approach of to Kieślowski's BLIND CHANCE (Kieślowski PL 1987 (1981)). Although, in Zhangke's film, the mirroring scenes reflect on the different mindsets and gender-specific circumstances of these two characters.

The mineworker searching for his daughter finds the place the address leads him to situated in that part which already has been flooded for the first level of the dam. In order to stay for continuing the search, he joins a group of men from different regions who came to the city for work. They introduce their home region to each other by showing pictures from the back of different banknotes. (Fig. 33) In contrast, the female character leading the middle part is presented as more distanced and observing. (Fig. 43) Her search starts from a privileged situation by having a friend who supports her search. The place the action is situated within, is well defined and part of the implicit dramaturgy. On the other hand, time is not shown as being definite progress in any of these episodes. There are days and nights but not a naturalistic protocol of the time these characters are spending in the city, or of how long it actually takes to find someone – or oneself.

The dam project and its foreseeable result induced Zhangke in making this film. That project is symbolising 'the great change' and promises a better future. The dam is going to be built in a landscape, which became iconic for the Tang Dynasty, the Golden Age of China.[311]

---

311 Zhangke 2008, p. 7

By sending two characters on a search into this town, Zhangke shows a kaleidoscope of characters, situations, the dialectic mixture of ancient and modern, ethereal and physical as well as the female and male experience of this city. Their experiences and points of view allow telling about the impact which the contemporary political situation has on social life and the interaction of very many people.[312] STILL LIFE is also categorised as 'ecocinema'.[313] A definition of eco-cinema summarises the meaning of epic movies (without mentioning epic) and emphasising that 'Such films invite viewers to refresh their perception of the world and the environment and to contemplate the world view in a new light different from usual mainstream commercial filmmaking.'[314] One feature of eco-cinema as well as of epic movies is to employ 'extended shots relatively still imagery as a way of asking that viewers slow down and explore what they're seeing.'[315]

In STILL LIFE, the main characters encounter a wide range of people and situations. Writer-director Zhangke aimed to give an impression of the simultaneity of beauty and ugliness, compassion and cruelty by showing extended shots of the landscape, the city, faces, and some still lifes of a different kind.[316] (Fig. 42 and 43) Aesthetically, he combines a detailed observation about the life in Fengjie with poetic moments. In two situations people are dancing to music that is not very danceable. One of them is located on a roof terrace above one of the new bridges built for the time after the flooding. The other one happens after the wife and husband met each other again after having been separated for two years. This is situated at a provisory bank in front of a viewing spot simulating the new level of the river after the dam is finished. They are also dancing to such a of music, which doesn't have a rhythm which one can dance at. (Fig. 44, 45)

Zhangke also integrates fantastic moments in a realistic setting. From time to time a Ufo appears, and a landmark building transforms into a rocket and flies off. These poetic interventions visualise how surreal life became as a result of the transformation process in China.

---

312 Zhangke 2008, p. 7
313 Lu 2017, p. 5
314 Ibid., p. 3
315 MacDonald 2004, p. 115
316 Zhangke 2008

Fig. 44: STILL LIFE   Fig. 45: STILL LIFE

Narrating a Life – The Biographic Film

Human beings are always interested in the life of other human beings. Hence, biographies are central to the traditions of storytelling. Biographic narrations, on the one hand, originates from myths and legends as well as from stories about biblical figures, on the other hand they are part of family life. The distinction between fantastic and authentic biographic storytelling results from the importance of the time in which the story takes place. Mythical stories happen regardless of real time, the time of the story presented is less directed and hence of direct impact but eternal. Epic narrations are linked to time proceeding, reacting to the chronology of events as they happen over time. But one does not have to narrate these in that chronological order.[317] A biographical epic flows with time.

For a work that is epically narrated, one can select one or more episodes from a biography that best expresses the theme for which the portrait is representative. One can arrange these biographical sequences based on dramaturgical rules introduced above. One can implement a Leitmotif to connect the fragments. That enables arranging them in non-linear order, and naturally one can tell the story of a life chronologically in time. The chosen dramaturgy and consequently, the rhythm too depend on sujet, plot, and overall theme. The form is composed to pronounce the purpose.[318] The biography can be that of a legendary character like ROBIN HOOD (Scott 2010), a character from the Bible – The PASSION OF THE CHRIST (Gibson, USA 2004), ESTHER

---

317 Carrière & Bonitzer 1999, p. 152
318 Cf. Balázs 2001, p. 77

(Mertes, I/G/USA 1999), or a Hindi Goddess or other personifications of power. It can tell about a person of particular interest from literature or history as CITIZEN KANE (WELLES, USA 1941), THE LAST TYCOON (Kazan, USA 1976), MOLIERE (Mnouchkine F 1978), ELISABETH (Kapur, UK 1998), MACBETH (Kurzel, UK/F/USA 2015) or fictional characters representing a particular social-historic period MADELEINE (Lean, UK 1950). A biographical film portrays a person or a group of people who, because of their position, status, character or historical, cultural, legendary significance, are ideally suited to embody a particular context.

One well-known example is CITIZEN KANE (Welles, USA 1941). In the first sequence, Orson Wells begins the story with a moment which resembles the concept of establishing a secret. What does the dying Kane refer to when mentioning 'Rosebud'? The first sequence is an associative montage combining different shapes of fences and shows a palace, which looks like a crossover of *Schwanstein Castle* and *Taj Mahal*.

An older man alone in a pompous room. He holds a snow globe in his hand and says 'Rosebud'. The snow globe falls and breaks, and a nurse comes to fold his hands over his breast. The man is dead. With this sequence, we have the impression of a man with an eclectic taste, who must be wealthy nonetheless alone. With the next sequence, a newsreel informs about Kane's career and what a respected person he has been. A journalist, Joseph Cotton (Jedediah Leland), wants to get to know more about Kane. When the journalist heard of Kane's last word, he is keen to find out what it stands for. Searching for an answer to this question, he acts as an epic self. The journalist is the central character of the investigation and hence a character equivalent to the 'central self' as introduced in chapter two. The inquiry of the journalist is organised in a way to determine the perspective and succession of events. Thus, Kane's biography is told in episodes, following the steps the journalist takes or material he has access to. By having an investigating journalist as the protagonist, it becomes plausible to organise the events in a more associative and fragmented way. Through the craft of his cinematographer Gregg Toland, who therefore got a credit next to Welles, the movie gains a strong visual metaphoric narration, which shows context and atmosphere and supports its associative dramaturgy. By using this metaphoric style Welles comments concurrently on the biography of Kane (Orson Welles, Sonny Bupp, Buddy Swan) and reflects on historical and social circumstances as well as the media industry. Given this dramaturgical composition, episodes can be arranged non-chronologically but in a thematical order, to give a consecutive understanding of how Citizen Kane developed into the person he was known as.

Another exemplary movie is LAWRENCE OF ARABIA (Lean, UK 1962). This movie is based on the memoir of the person who is remembered as 'Lawrence of Arabia'. The film begins with an overture. Director David Lean wanted to immerse the audience in a unique atmosphere before the movie starts. Maurice Jarre composed the music for this movie and thus introduced the leitmotif in this overture.

The movie then begins with a prelude sequence. Lawrence (Peter O'Toole) starts off on a ride on his motorcycle. The scenery is typical of rural Britain. The accident, which happens at the end of this sequence, is implicitly announced when early in his ride he has to drive through an area of road work where a sign is signalling 'Warning! Danger!'. After we have watched Lawrence crossing this area, he drives fast and faster, his view blurring. In the next shot, we see him lose control over his motorcycle when two postmen on their bicycles approach him on his side of the road. The accident consequently leads to Lawrence's funeral. When adapting Lawrence's memoirs, the screenwriters added this scene. This allows introducing a first impression of the central character. And, on the implicit level, Welles establishes an association with the country life in the United Kingdom, a familiar looking region, that also signalizes belonging, Britishness, and a civilisation grown from tradition.

The second sequence shows the end of his funeral ceremony. On the explicit level, it results from the event shown in the prelude. Implicit, it tells of the importance of his life and work for the Empire, of his connection to the capital and the significance of the St Paul's Cathedral. These two scenes are essential to establish the character in a British context, to focus the perspective of the viewer to his character and the events, to contextualise his actions and behaviour throughout the following story.

The very first dialogue of the movie addresses the camera. The person, who speaks first, is glancing towards Lawrence's bust framed by flags, which also informs us about the year the event happens, that is 1935. The man is standing in the cathedral together with a priest, while other people are leaving the church.

"He was the most extraordinary man I ever knew."
"Do you knew him well?", asks the priest.
"I knew him," the man nods.
"Well, nil nisi bonum.[319] Did he really deserve a place in here?"[320]

With a travelling shot over the façade of St Paul's Cathedral, the action moves outside. On the stairs, a journalist is approaching some of those who are leaving the ceremony. He is asking about Colonel Lawrence, and thus, introducing his military background. The first person who is asked about Lawrence, answers 'No, no. I didn't know him well, you know.' The next one describes him as 'a scholar, a poet, and a mighty worrier.' After the journalist goes away, he whispers to his companion that Lawrence was also 'the most shameless exhibitionist since Barnum and Bailey'.[321] This remark provokes the outrage of another person who has to admit that he didn't know him either. The next person asked, answers as well that he didn't know him but once shook his hand, and that he, Lawrence 'had some minor function on my staff in Cairo'. The ironic character of the scene results from this interplay between people who admire him without knowing the man in person and those who knew him. That way, the character Lawrence is introduced as a personality who can be well presented as a modern center figure. Such a person is, as mentioned above, not a person to be considered as utterly positive. In the first scene of the biographical story, he is introduced as an untypical character. The audience may still reflect on the question asked shortly before: Does he deserve to be seen as a hero honoured with a place in St. Paul's Cathedral?[322] Implicit it may as well reflect on the question of what makes a person or character a hero?

The situation the story evolves from takes place in Egypt during World War I. A war, as mentioned above, is understood to be one ideal form to

---

319   "Of the dead, [say] nothing but good"
320   Zinnemann, UK/F 1973, 1:40 min
321   B&B were a circus company also known as the Ringling brothers advertising themselves as 'The Greatest Show on Earth'.
322   For more than 1,400 years, this Cathedral dedicated to St Paul has stood at the highest point in the City. It is frequently at the centre of national events, and home to a spectacular array of art. https://www.stpauls.co.uk/history-collections/history

start an epic narration. Due to the war, Lawrence is sent on a special mission. Challenged by the influence of historical, cultural and climatic circumstances, this figure is shown as forced to demonstrate his character traits, and the story unfolds accordingly. Consequently, this figure makes decisions that are very much influenced by historical conditions, cultural traditions, and the topography of the area the action takes place. He is presented as being of partial influence on the progress of the events but not in full control of the overall situation. Correspondingly, the character can emotionally overreact, do stupid things, behave bravely and badly, is allowed to make mistakes, to hesitate and to express a very peculiar worldview. The story spans a few years and a vast territory. Although the inner narration is told chronologically, it had to be arranged episodically to focus on the most relevant parts of the events Lawrence is involved in. In the end, the question asked in the beginning still has to be answered, and the reactions may be as varied as the voices interviewed in the exposition-sequence.

For her biographic movie MOLIÈRE (Mnouchkine F 1978), Ariane Mnouchkine chose an aesthetically very different style than the directors mentioned above.

Mnouchkine's movie begins with a shot facing a stage that signals earlier times. No music, no sound design. The focus of this scene is on the visual power of the deserted stage. As a visual counterpoint, a candle is shining in the back, in the area usually not accessible to the audience. As if to confirm the first observation, a woman wearing clothing of an earlier period crosses the theatre. She brings a dress to the man backstage. One can hear nothing but her shoes clattering on the floor. She enters the area at the back at the stage, but the camera stays in front of the open door and thus framing the portrait of a senior man sitting at a desk. He writes, coughs. Still observed from the framing distance, the man rises and changes clothes with the help of the woman. No one speaks, he continues coughing. On her way back, another man approaches, asking her about the man's well-being. She answers that 'it is bad, he is coughing, crumbling. It is a bad day.' The man looks worried. The others are in the church, 'Madelaine died a year ago today'. The two whisper. The actor expresses his thought that the other man should not go on stage today; he is too sick. The man in the background, Molière, answers that he is in perfect health but wants to be left in peace. They have to start on time: 'or you'll have to perform without me'. The woman repeats that this is a bad day; both are leaving towards the opposite direction of the stage, into a dark area in the back. With a shot repeating the very first one, the title starts, music as well, and a female narrator informs the audience that Molière died on February 17, 1673, after the fourth performance of *Le Malade Imaginaire [The imaginary invalid]*. The scenery changes with the following information about Molière. The inner, from here chronologically arranged story begins with a situation which happened when Molière was ten years old. This situation is a theatrical-like game Jean-Baptiste is part of. This situation takes place in an attic, reflecting on social disparities amongst the children playing with each other. It, as well, resembles the style of theatre performances of that time. The film follows through Molière's life, focussing on different episodes of his life which formed his interest in theatre, his skills as an actor, becoming head of a travelling theatre company and the famous author as well as the partner of Madelaine. The short dialogue about Madelaine's death can be understood as a variant of an establishing moment raising the interest of the audience. No one mentions how she died, but that this anniversary of her death causes Moliere's bad mood becomes obvious. The attention of the audience is directed here to an individual faith as well. The movie is not just about the famous artist. Mnouchkine creates this biographic movie as a presentation of historical developments and everyday situations, which influenced this excellent observer who immediately picks up the performativity of every situation. Therefore, the film aesthetic emphasises the performative character of all moments of life, no matter how seemingly minor or influential they are.

Dramaturgical Aspects of Multi-Perspective Narratives

Multi-perspective works represent a further variant of the possibilities listed above. Its definite peculiarity, as the term already expresses, consists of the opportunity to show different perspectives on an event. In this sense, multi-perspective narration combines aspects of epic with an episodic narrative. In this dramaturgical model, the episodes can be designed differently from in the above examples. In particular, the movement through time and space depends on the narrated point of view of the acting figures.

One of the movies that became influential and famous for using a multi-perspective narration is 羅生門 RASHŌMON (Kurosawa J 1950). In his ground-breaking movie, Kurosawa reflects on perception, experience, and memory. On the explicit level of narration, the plot is situated in the 11th century. On the implicit level, the movie refers to experiences of World War II and its aftermath. The theme comprehends the relationship of truth and falsehood, of assumption and awareness as well as of that of the relation of object and subject. The figures appear in one of the sequences as an object of the narration, in the other as the narrator, and in a third one just as an observer, neither object nor subject. Kurosawa interconnects these three levels of the narration with three different places. The incident causing the action is an ambush on a clearing in a grove. In a gatehouse, where all figures take shelter from heavy rain, the main narration takes place. And a tribunal investigating the event is situated in a bare room. The sparse set design directs the focus onto the characters, which are acting uncommunicatively and introverted, at least for an European eye. Every figure presents their interpretation of how they remember the assault. The incident interconnects the delineations of events.

Nevertheless, every witness, as well as the victim, gives a different statement. But every report seems to be convincing and plausible, coming from the perspective of the individual narrator. Thus, the audience must decide which view to accept as most probable or how to relate to the situation at all.

Inspired by Kurosawa's movie, by novels using a multi-perspective structure, as well as by scholarly work on poly-perspective narration, in film dramaturgy as well as scriptwriting more multi-perspective movies have been produced. The multi-perspective narrative has its roots in stage drama as well as in polyphonic music.

Polyphonic is a term established in music practice and theory since 1300. Polyphonicity is also determined as "many-voicedness." Most of the music of the Middle Ages is polyphone, as in the compositions by Giovanni Pierluigi da Palestrina (1525–1594), Lassus, de Monte, amongst others; Bach for example for the Baroque period, and so on.[323] 'Western polyphony emerged in a charged relation with Christian theology but has become ubiquitous: beginning as music suitable for divine minds, for gods and angels, in time polyphony became a defining attribute of human personhood.'[324] When listening to music

323 Pesic 2017, position 414
324 Ibid., position 349

the audience had to connect different voices. Station theatre, that emerged at approximately the same period as polyphonic music was reflected on in scholarly writing about music, was and is multi-perspective and episodic as well, as the theatre performance of the *Théâtre du Soleil* shows in 1789 (Mnouchkine, F 1974).

In literary theory, narratives told by various voices spread over several levels and situations are called poly- or multi-perspective.[325] Different variations are possible in composing the dramaturgy for a poly-perspective narration. The action can be lead or commented upon by two or more protagonists who influence the plot and/or part of the chain of events. These characters can appear together or alternate, in some narrations at the same time and in the same situation where nevertheless having/representing a different perspective - as in SHUTTER ISLAND (SCORSESE, USA 2010).

In HILARY AND JACKIE (Tucker, UK 1998), for example, the story of two sisters, who become competitive musicians, is told. After both of them are introduced, every scene presents the perspective from one of the sisters, which alternates although the story progresses chronologically. As a politic-thriller, in which time has dramaturgical impact, SYRIANA (Gaghan, USA 2005) is chronologically narrated although it's episodic and multi-perpspective as well. The story unfolding is presented from two independent perspectives, with characters who never meet in person. A theme connects them, moreover in dialectic correspondence to each other, with a bomb as physical artefact intertwining the different levels of narration.

As the third opportunity, one can arrange the multi-perspective narration as a collage. In this case, episodes of metaphoric meaning complement the perspective of the protagonist, episodes which are not presented through a character – it can be observations of landscape, nature, or abstract audio-visual interludes. In a modern movie, these episodes can be designed retrospective or introspective.

It is also possible that the main character is presented experiencing the world as fragmented and hence has to deal with different fragments

---

325 Röttgers & Schmitz-Emans 1999; Genette writes about "anachrony", but his theories are very much bound to written text being of two-dimensional narration and thus are not fully applicable to the time-based art such as films. Genette 2010

and perspectives at once - as in THE TRACEY FRAGMENTS (McDonald, CDN 2007).

Another dramaturgical pattern enables one to tell the same story with multiple courses of events and endings and thus from different perspectives. This is a form, which Kieślowski chose for his movie PRZYPADEK [BLIND CHANCE] (Kieślowski, PL 1987 (1981)). Kieślowski tells a story in three resembling versions for which the beginning of the following one always starts from the end of the prior one. Every one of these versions reacts to the experiences, which the protagonist had during the action of the previous one. Thus, every new version seems to be a commentary on the last experience of the main character. In a dramaturgical pattern like this, in which multiple endings are possible, the invariable protagonist starts from a similar initial situation, although the course of events varies within interconnected variations. In this movie, space is identifiable, but time becomes relative or moves circularly. Kieślowski's movie was adapted for LOLA RENNT [LOLA RUNS] (Tykwer, 1998), and STILL LIFE (Zhangke, CH 2006) refers to it as well, amongst others.

These forms of poly-perspective narration imply a philosophical, modern approach to the world as described above. Mikhail Bakhtin's dialogue theory[326] supports this understanding. He writes amongst other arguments that the new artist has to deal with a heritage he may react against in order to become able to adapt it in a creative approach. Artists must orientate themselves and their work within the tradition. The challenges for the artists are to express themselves extrinsically in an inherited tongue. Mayakovsky, Meyerhold, and Eisenstein inspired Bakhtin's philosophical reflections on artistic practice and opportunities. When parts of his works were translated into English and consequently intensely discussed in the Anglo-American world during the 1960s and 70s, many directors and writers were inspired to produce multi-perspective narrated movies.

These traditions of multi-perspective narrated movies also have an analogy to the 'systemic design' as it is practiced in psychology. The change of perspective enables us to consider an individual drama from the standpoint of all persons involved. That change of perspective is intended to

---

326 Bachtin 1986, 2011

establish a symbolic interaction, understood as essential to all human and social communication.

Babel

Title and trailer of Babel (Iñárritu, F/USA/MEX 2006) refer to *Genesis* 11,7–9, of which it is a variation[327] (which has different translations and adaptations either): 'In the beginning are the Lord's people from all parts of the world. Spoken one language. Nothing they propose was impossible for them.'[328]

The destruction of communication occurred as a reaction to people's efforts to jointly build a tower that one can understand as an act of self-empowerment.[329] The Bible tells us that the universal language of the time was Hebrew – until the destruction of the Tower of Babel.[330]

The movie and the array of events begin with the introduction of a physical item, a rifle. On the explicit level, this rifle connects everything which will happen afterwards. Implicit, though, the theme of love, trust, family, and interpersonal communication defines every episode of the movie. The concept of belonging to, founding or securing a family is the core of American thinking[331] and hence of 'American dramaturgy'.[332]

On the explicit level, the rifle connects everything and is, therefore, the centre of the action of the very first sequence. The scenery is a barren landscape, mountains, stones, some grass, dust, and wind. An older man, Hassan (Abdelkader Bara), sells the rifle to another man, Abdullah (Mustapha Rachidi). Their two sons in their early teens, Ahmed (Said Tarchani) and Yussef (Bubker Ait El Said), are goatherds. They need the rifle to keep the

---

327 Come, let us go down, and there confound their language, that they may not understand one another's speech. So the LORD scattered them abroad from thence upon the face of all earth. Therefore was the name of it called Babel; because the LORD did there confound the language of all the earth; and from thence did the LORD scatter them abroad upon the face of all the earth.

328 Paramount, 2006

329 Liss, Boeckler, & Landthaler 2011, p. 26

330 Hahn & Hahn 1996, p. 22/23

331 Cf. Fiedler 1992

332 Cf. Belton 2009; Bentley 1967; Frenz 1962, pp. 8–11; Stutterheim 2015, pp. 153–159

jackals away. These two sons are introduced as being different from each other, resembling Esau and Jacob. The elder appears traditional and less talented. The younger is self-confident, quick. He seems to be less religious but a better shooter and a gifted liar. His counterpart is Chieko (Rinko Kikuschi). Both are striving to have their first sexual experiences. And both characters are challenging the people around them, leading the action of their narrative level/episodes.

The Arabic family, whose patriarch buys the rifle, and the family of the American tourists, Richard (Brad Pitt) and Susan (Kate Blanchet), are dramaturgically arranged as antagonistic entities. The Arab family is introduced as a traditional functioning family; the American's as a modern couple who travel to overcome some problem in their relationship. In their first scene, they are sitting in an eatery somewhere in an Arabic country. In this scene, Susan asks her husband why they are there. On the explicit level, this question is directed to her husband, who might have arranged this trip. Implicit this is a more general question, also directed towards the audience, introducing a sub-theme, which becomes more apparent when, after a short beat of contemplation, the husband answers: 'To forget everything, to be alone.'[333] This short answer is connected to the theme of life and death, and consequently central for the implicit dramaturgy and essential meaning.

In this situation in the restaurant, the character of Susan is introduced. She overreacts to everything. She does not trust the food or the ice cubes for her cola, although many tourists frequent the restaurant. She reacts dismissively to her husband, who seems to stoically try to cheer her up, or at least wants to be near her. We learn that they have a nanny, Amelia (Adrianna Barraza), who takes care of their two children Debbie (Elle Fanning) and Mike (Nathan Gamble). Amelia often lives with the family, as shown in the episode before. Later, Amelia describes her relationship with the children as strong as if they were her own: 'Sir, I raised these kids since they were born. I take care of them day and night. I feed them break-fast, lunch and dinner. I play with them. Mike and Debbie are like my own children.'[334]

---

333 Iñárritu Babel – Screenplay 2005, p 16
334 Ibid., p 113

We learn that Amelia is a mother herself. Her adult son, Luis (Robert 'Bernie' Esquivel), gets married in one of the episodes. Her nephew (Gael García Bernal) is picking her up at the house of the American family. An extended family celebrates the wedding as a big party. In these surroundings, Amelia is shown as a respected woman, also a desirable one.

The incident starting the action happens shortly afterwards, when the two boys test how far the rifle can reach – the elder son, Ahmed, shoots at a car and fails. He suggests that Yussef should aim at the bus coming into sight that very moment. He does. And hits. The coach stops. We learn that tourists from different parts of the world travel together in this coach. One can interpret the tourists on that coach as descendants of all the people who are send all over the world, consequently speaking different languages. Susan is hit. The boys are shocked about the hit and hide the rifle. The attempt to shoot jackals to secure the family income transforms into dramatic action, involving people in different parts of the world and their families. The incident resulting in an array of events brings the characteristics of society and individuals to the surface and is the dramaturgical principle of the epic narration. Because it is an American tourist who is shot, it is immediately predicted that is must have been a terrorist attack. The Moroccan guide, Anwar (Mohamed Akhzam), offers immediate help. The other tourists in the bus demand to continue with their trip, which seems to be a like a sideline and not really relevant. It is since moment in which a 'war-like' act forces the members of a social group, who in this case travel together in a bus through a foreign country, makes every one of them show their real character.

When the couple arrives in the house of Anwar, another family is introduced. Anwar's home is what we would call today a multi-generational house. He is the father of five children. Asked by Richard how many wives he is married to, Anwar answers that he only can afford one.

In association with the shot Susan, the Japanese father-daughter relationship is introduced as a reduced family. We are informed that the wife/mother committed suicide a few months ago. The daughter Chieko (Rinko Kikuschi) is a deaf-mute teenager. In the construction of the plot, Amelia and her son Yasijuro Wataya (Kôji Yakusho) are juxtaposed with that father and his daughter. Both parent-child constellations face challenges of different forms of distance and closeness. The very different family relationships form the implicit texture on which the narrative on the explicit level can develop in a way that some perceive as independent and unrelated.

The movie is narrated in episodes, which are not organised chronologically but following the concept arranging the American and Arabic family as antagonistic. An ensemble of characters tells the story. The family introduced as relatively well functioning, in the beginning, is destroyed, resulting from the incident. That of the American couple is shown as dysfunctional at the beginning. They becom a loving couple towards the end, probably healed from their wounds of having lost a child recently. They promise each other and the audience never to leave their children alone ever again. The storyline regarding Amelia ends with her being sent back to Mexico and welcomed by her son; thus, she becomes reunified with her biological family. The shattered father and daughter are shown as comforting each other.

Thematically, all of the episodes are organised along the theme of love and death. Explicit, the use of the rifle interconnects the events. The episodes are connected in an associative way known from poetic cinema and avant-garde art. For example, the boys, Yussef and Ahmed, hide behind a stone, and this is followed by a similar scene, of the American children playing hide and seek in the kitchen in San Diego. Then, the narration moves from the kitchen in San Diego back to the eatery in Morocco.

The editing is organised similarly after the shot that hits Susan. Here, the narration jumps into the situation on a volleyball court in Japan, where a throw was misjudged – and so forth.

The story is arranged circularly. At the end of the movie, the phone conversation from the second scene is shown from the opposite angle, like mirrored. At the beginning of the film, Amelia and little Mike were shown answering Richard's call, whereas in the mirrored scene, the very same call happens; now the audience observes Richard.

The character who goes with the name Richard is the central protagonist. He is the white male hero, who does everything to rescue his wife - from her depression at first to the life-threatening accident replacing the conflict. He also takes care of the children at home, keeps everything going. From a dramaturgical approach, every episode or storyline has its main central character – Yussef, Amelia, Richard, Chieko, who together form an ensemble. Although all these characters are of some influence to the progressing story, again, the male protagonist is central within the overall action. Hidden within the attempted multi-perspective and non-linear structure is the main principle of Hollywood-movies, in which it is a core dramaturgical aspect that the white male hero must rescue his wife and his family above everything else. This aspect is core to the story told in Babel. In the end, the antagonist, Yussef hands himself in to the police to stop the shooting of his family. The characters of Amelia and Chieko are important for their episodes and are told together with family matters as well, but their actions are not of substantial influence to the main narrative.

Ensemble Films

For writing and directing ensemble films, one should choose a multi-perspective narrative. In ensemble films, three or more protagonists are arranged in such a way as to have an equal dramatic influence on the plot and all elements of the action.

The decision or habits these characters are supplied with by the writer/director to enable them to act or not must be influenced by and influencing the ongoing narration. Regardless of how the story unfolds, we experience the film narrative as an eyewitness. It can be a situation seemingly unchanged in which only times moves on. Dialogical situations as well as metaphoric design connect different levels of narration. The plot develops from the interaction of these narrative threads.

One example for an ensemble film, already mentioned above in the paragraph introducing the center figure, is POLISSE (Maïwenn, F 2011). The action of this movie takes place in Paris and is connected with a police department. A group of different characters established as investigators in a special unit *"Brigade de Protection de Mineurs"*, a group investigating child abuse and violence against children, form the ensemble. A photographer, the center figure, is appointed to produce a photo-reportage about the work of this unit. The six members of the ensemble, every one of them representing different traits, status, gender, are arranged as dialogic pairs. This way, the movie tells about the life in Paris, across all social classes, from every day challenges to general problems.

In LIFE ACCORDING TO AGFA (Dayan, ISR 1993), a day in Tel Aviv is a portrait of a society. A small (invented) bar in the centre of the city gives the 'point of perspective'. Every member of the ensemble is one way or the other connected to this bar. It is a metaphor as well as a representation of a microcosmos of Israel of that time. The name of the bar, "Barbie", is an ironic reference to the satirical nickname of a famous mental health institution in Israel. The centre figure is the owner of the bar, Daliah (Gila Almagor). She has a daughter, going with the name Mimi, who admires Japan martial arts movies and loves Pizza. The group of people working at or visiting the bar give a cross-section of society. Young to old, from civilians of all kind - Israeli, Palestinian, Israeli Arab, migrants, a detective - to the military. Several small events happen in this bar, connecting the ensemble during the night and thus enfolding a condensed portrait of society. Dayan 'made it clear that "Agfa" embodies something of a Hegelian view of the majority culture, and talks about "a pyramid that starts from our national loneliness", and involves "a type of national suicide."' It became 'one of Israeli cinema's most important films'.[335] In this movie, the writer-director Assi Dayan establishes a stable chronotopos, very classical, which gives structure to a texture of events of which some are happening simultaneously and develop into episodically individual storylines. Some of them are influencing each other explicitly in a direct course of action; others are implicitly intertwined.

Often in movies that are produced in the Anglo-American hemisphere, thus closer to the hero-driven tradition, a group of characters is organised around a central character, as a central self. An excellent example to explain this particular dramaturgical approach, is BRASSED OFF (Herman, UK 1996) and more recent and with a more complex structure emerging from this principle GAME OF THRONES (Benioff & Weiss, USA 2011–2019), to mention just a few.

In BRASSED OFF, the centre figure is the leader of the brass band Danny (Pete Postlethwaite). The brass band stands symbolically for the mining industry which is about to be shut down. Members of the band and their individual stories form a portrait of a community shaped by this industry

---

335 n.n., 2011

and dependent on the pit. Danny's son Phil (Stephen Tompkinson) struggles with saving his family from harm and his finances from catastrophe; Andy (Ewan McGregor) a young mineworker playing the trumpet, and other band members are having different private problems alongside the closure of the pit. And there is Gloria Mulland (Tara Fitzgerald), grand-daughter of one of the former bandleaders. She inherited not only the flugelhorn from her grandfather but also talent. On the other hand, she returned to her home town to work for the management of the pit. Writer-director Herman connects the ensemble of different characters through the brass band. The competition the band participates in connects the lives of all these characters on the explicit level and allows emphasising the dramaturgically central situations by a cinematic conflict rooted in a performance of the band.

The Road Movie

Road movies are a sub-category of films movies and in most cases are episodically narrated. Some of them are ensemble films, some multi-perspective, others tell about one or two characters. Their main feature is to be arranged along a journey.

The epic movie is proceeding through time; the road movie is travelling through space. Time here is related to the journey and the means of carriage. Undertaking a journey as a motif for the structure of an episodic narration refers back to early storytelling. Initially, often it is a hero who travels through a world and experiences adventures, has romantic (or erotic) scary or amusing encounters, which the episodes being connected by the traveller.[336] Travel narratives can be situated in the imagination or as dreams, diaries, poems, novels, drama, as well as experimental, documentary or fictional films. Narrations telling of a journey can be traced back to the *Odyssey*[337] or the *Mahabharata*[338], the dream travels in the traditions of the indigene people, fairy tales, and more. The critical feature for this dramaturgical pattern is again that the narrated travel has to be plausible, believable and following a logic based on a theme, although not necessarily

---

336 Cf. Burdorf et al. 2007, pp. 640–642
337 Homer, 8. Jh. v.u.Z.
338 Smith 2009

true in the sense of being factually correct. Again, time and space must correlate but don't have to be naturalistic. Either one or the other should be as close to the perception of reality as possible. Our memory is not accurate either; we don't remember elements of a journey that don't contain information necessary to understanding or remembering this particular voyage. This operational principle of the human mind, which is primed by cultural traditions and language patterns, provides a good orientation for the dramaturgical approach to design such a film.

A journey as motif and explicit part of the action can be found since the early years of film history – to start with L'ARRIVÉE D'UN TRAIN EN GARE DE LA CIOTAT [THE ARRIVAL OF A TRAIN] (Lumière & Lumière, F 1896) by the Lumière brothers or THE GREAT TRAIN ROBBERY (Porter, USA 1903). In the US American history of cinema, the road movie is a central genre since the early years of movie production. It entails motifs of discovering and conquering new land, unknown territory, as well as intellectual, ethic, and technological advancement.[339] Bela Balász emphasised in regard to road movies that a journey is an experience of profound impact.[340] Protagonists, who embark on a journey, are crossing a line. They venture into the unknown, into alien, foreign or alternative regions. Crossing different areas or arriving somewhere else they have to orientate themselves within an order and/or circumstances, different to those they are used to. Consequently, in situations different from their everyday life – as well as of that of the audience – the protagonists have to prove themselves in extraordinary circumstances, therefore showing their true character traits. These challenges, experiences, and achievements allow the character to develop. A road movie can also tell about imaginary travels or regions. It isn't necessary that that only one person makes the journey, it is – in particular in modern movies – possible to arrange a group of characters travelling. These can be connected in one dialectic way or the other, such as family, perchance, because they have to work together, they are a combat unit or a crew. When a group goes on a journey together, every one of these protagonists can represent different approaches, aspects of a character, or a diverse world and hence can embody people of different socio-cultural

---

339 Cohan & Hark 1997
340 Balázs 2001, p. 76

priming, education, or/and status. During the journey, they may encounter challenging situations and/or figures.

In a road movie, the route supports the storyline. The motif of travelling enables one to connect a variety of episodes which don't have to be successive. The journey allows for the writer/director to abstract reality or to transform a theme into conceptual space, in which events act as metaphors representing the overall plot, the ultimate meaning. Time becomes a power influencing the journey and has an effect on the unfolding events as well as on the rhythm of the narration, the cinematography, sound design, and the editing.

The motif of a journey is essential to very many movies, amongst others can be mentioned here STAGE COACH (Ford, 1939), THE WIZARD OF OZ (Fleming, USA 1939), EASY RIDER (Hopper, USA 1969); LA STRADA (Fellini, 1954), TICKETS (Olmi, Kiarostami, & Loach, 2005), STILL LIFE (Zhangke, CH 2006), Коктебель [Roads to Koktebel] (Khlebnikov & Popogrebsky, R 2003) and Science Fiction movies as CONTACT (Robert Zemeckis, USA 1997), GRAVITY (Cuarón, UK/USA 2013).

Also, documentary filmmaker often use the concept of a road movie to structure their work, for example, TURKSIB (Turin, USSR 1929), NIGHT MAIL (Watt & Wright, UK 1936), THE NET (Dammbeck, D 2003), THE END OF TIME (Mettler, CDN/CH 2012).

Taking characters and audiences on a journey is always an adventure and also entertaining when the journey invites everyone to explore new terrain, but the travel must be appropriately organised so as not to loose companions on the way.

TV Series

In general, all series productions combine the principles of explicit and implicit dramaturgy, epic and episodic dramaturgy as introduced above. Dramaturgical basic rules apply as well. Thus, the series is a variation, for which additional aspects to the dramaturgical tradition emerge. During TV history, different kinds of series have been produced, and therefore a diverse dramaturgical tradition have evolved. TV series are exceedingly crucial for broadcasters or providers to attract and keep an audience bound to the provider. Series guarantee a good part of their income.

In this chapter, I will give an overview of the most common dramaturgical forms in the western world which can be applied to TV, web-distributed, or Auteur series. These are not restricted to drama or fictional productions. Documentary series made for broadcasting or online distribution follow the same dramaturgical pattern.

The features on in this chapter, in addition to the aspects introduced above, are those of the horizontal and the vertical dramaturgy, which are fundamental to the dramaturgy of a series.

Horizontal Dramaturgy

The horizontal dramaturgy gives a series and each season its central narrative and thus a solid backbone. The horizontal dramaturgy supports the narrative strand or a continuous motif or pattern, whereby the episodes are related to each other in such a way that there is a constant progression. The continuing narration has to be developed following the principles of epic storytelling, organised as an episodic structure. For these productions, too, the overall action is determined by a theme that relates all sections of the storyline to one another.

Also, the horizontal narration is most likely driven by the activities of a protagonist, a pair of main characters, or an ensemble around a 'centre figure', as introduced above. These protagonists can be detectives, doctors, investigators, prisoners, lawyers, or just a family or neighbourhood, or an animal with or without its human friend. The horizontal dramaturgy can span an on-going investigation, as in MIAMI

VICE (Michael Mann, USA 1984–1990), FORBYDELSEN (Sveistrup, DK/N/S/D 2007–2012) or THE NIGHT MANAGER (Bier, UK 2016). In most cases, it also tells about a period in the life of a person, or of a community, which serves the moment of familiarity. Therefore, the primary plot thread can include a love story or the up and downs of a family moved either by circumstances or the profession of the main character, or a combination of those.

For example, a series can be thematically connected by a presenter or the main character - as I LOVE LUCY (Ball, USA 1951–1957). Series can be composed in a structure that enables the telling of an on-going story of the protagonist and his or her family as in LASSIE (Maxwell USA 1954–1973), LITTLE HOUSE ON THE PRAIRIE (Hanalis, USA 1974–1983), DALLAS (Jacobs USA 1978–1991), as well as WALLANDER (Mankell, S/D/DK/N/FIN 2005–2013;) and its adaptation (UK/S/USA/D 2008–2016).

Series productions can have a continuously evolving storyline in which one event follows another logically, as we know it from MIAMI VICE (Michael Mann, USA 1984–1990), DALLAS (Jacobs, USA 1978–1991), DYNASTY (Shapiro & Shapiro, USA 1981–1989), MILLENNIUM (Carter, USA 1996–1999), BREAKING BAD (Gilligan, 2008–2013), SHERLOCK (Gatiss, Moffat, and Thompson 2010–2017), MYSTERY ROAD (Sen, AUS 2013) to mention a few. In these series, consistency is determined by personal stories of the main characters.

One variation to this fundamental principle that transforms the classical drama into a series is the model in which the main character has a family life that supports the horizontal dramaturgy. Such a basic storyline holds in addition to the collective narration and allows extending a series for more seasons, although every season is triggered by a new incident and thus new characters are involved. Examples for this are REGENESIS (CAN 2004–2008) or FORBRYDELSEN (Sveistrup 2007–2012), THE CODE (Birse, AUS 2014–219), and HATUFIM (Raff 2009–2012) as well as many more US-productions. This principle is echoed in series in which a team that is set up as an ensemble replaces the family. In these productions, personal stories enrich the leading strand of the narrative emotionally, as in CSI (Zuicker USA 2000–2015), NCIS (Bellissario and McGill USA 2003-) or BONES (Hanson USA 2005–2017) for example.

Popular examples for long-running series that follow this principle are LASSIE, BONANZA (Dortort, USA 1959–1973), LITTLE HOUSE ON THE PRAIRIE (Hanalis, USA 1974–1983), DALLAS (Jacobs, 1978–1991) and DYNASTY (Shapiro & Shapiro, USA 1981–1989), CORONATION STREET (Warren, UK 1960-), to mention a few.

Protagonists of modern TV series are most often situated in a particularly challenging situation and therefore need a character trait, which distinguishes them from ordinary people, although they seem to be close to being 'one of us'. At least one character within an ensemble is designed as close as possible to the 'ordinary people' within the audience – as Watson (Martin Freeman) in SHERLOCK (Gatiss, Moffat, & Thompson, 2010–2015) or the characters of the pregnant Angela Burr (Olivia Coleman) and that of Jonathan Pine (Tom Hiddleston) who becomes almost accidentally a hero in THE NIGHT MANAGER. However, also the main characters of such series as SCOTT & BAILEY (Wainwright & Taylor, UK 2011–2016) appear as close to life, but their stories are nonetheless distinct from the everyday life of members of the audience.

In other productions, the storyline can emerge from a theme. A theme as a point of convergence can be presented through a chain of events, as with BLACK MIRROR (Brooker USA 2011-). In this production, every episode seems to present a different story. Nevertheless, all of these are interconnected by the overall theme, aesthetic, and rhythm.

The dramaturgical concept for the horizontal narration has to consider the rhythm of the episodes and their inner structure. Episodes function equally as segments of a season as a well as short independent dramatic narrations. For a season one must respect the same fundamental dramaturgical rules as for a series. A season needs a consistent dramaturgy to give the single episode its meaning and narrative quality to the overall plot. That aesthetic aspect is, in turn, one part of the series as such. Therefore, a season needs an underlying storyline that can be extended if this production is successful and to be continued. Depending on the circumstances of the production, a series can be created to have a particular number of seasons. Producer and broadcaster decide after every season whether to proceed or not. Thus, a season needs to have a plausible ending for the given plot. If there is a chance of getting the opportunity to continue, it is recommended not to let the main character die ahead of time.[341]

Horizontal dramaturgy contains the primary storyline for the whole season. In series made in the USA, and those mirroring that model, the personal story of the central character influences the progressing action. In contemporary series, the storyline of the central character is often intertwined with those of the ensemble. In those series which follow the European tradition of arranging a storyline and motivating characters, most often the theme dominates the plot. Hence, the incident or conflict that starts the action determines the dramaturgical and directorial approach.

Vertical Dramaturgy

A vertical dramaturgy is required for individual episodes and plot threads created for these. The basic dramaturgical concept of an episode corresponds to the dramaturgy requirements of episodic narration, as described in the previous chapters. The particular challenge for the creation of a series lies in combining dramaturgical components and premises. First of all, the narrative for each episode must be designed to serve the moments of familiarity and continuity. Since the end of the 1990s, it has become more and more customary to interweave three to five interrelated lines of action, each of which is dramaturgically composed as logical and credible in itself and merge them into one narrative. Accordingly, it is necessary to decide the order and correspondences of these strands of action. At least one of the conflicts and hence one of the strands should be resolved within the episode. As a result, one gets the impression of a certain unity and closeness. However, a series dramaturgy also requires the open end, the 'Cliff Hanger'. Such a situation can be established either as part the central plot, in the horizontal dramaturgy, in a subplot, or one of the vertical narratives that one can be drawn over more than one episode. In some series, a story within a story can be stretched over several episodes, as long as one of the plots that dominate the episode is closed at the end of the particular episode. A Cliff Hanger awakens the curiosity of the audience for the next

---

341 Cf. Dreher 2014

episode – or season. This principle serves to keep the audience interested in the series and thus binds them to the broadcaster or channel.

Auteur-Series and Visual Dramaturgy

Television productions were - and still are in some countries/broadcasting houses - primarily dominated by the spoken word, with not much effort put into visual narration and mostly with naturalistic mise-en-scène. In recent years, more and more series have been produced with higher demands, following a recognisable concept that does not only do justice to the particular genre and associated conventions. Many of them are labelled as 'Auteur-Series'. The difference, however, results from more a holistic aesthetic concept which includes a visual level of narrative.

One of the most influential series, in which the visual dramaturgy is as relevant to the development of the plot as the spoken dialogues, is MIAMI VICE (Mann 1984–1990). The use of colour dramaturgy in particular, but also the costume design was unusual and new for that time. It was complemented by referential music and sound design in the sense of postmodern aesthetics. Also new for a detective series was to organise the plot around two complementary characters within an ensemble, instead of the otherwise all dominating successful investigator.

About a decade later Lynch questioned the tradition of the TV series with TWIN PEAKS (Lynch USA 1990–91).

> 'Lynch's unbridled style of typical surrealism and oddities, bizarre characters and non-resolution of the crime-plot, Twin Peaks caused a sensation - never before in the cosmos of worldwide television had it been possible to do something as idiosyncratic and focussed on the personal preferences and visions of a director who had obviously been left largely free rein to develop his idea.'[342]

Today, high-quality television series are classified as artistically created and compared with the Nouvelle Vague in the cinema.[343] Many creative people who were previously working on cinema productions migrated to television series, particularly those produced independently or outside the traditional broadcasting system. The crises of the cinema make the new

---

342 Dreher 2010, p. 34
343 Ibid., p. 58

television attractive for creative people, as some critics summarize: 'TV can be programmed for niche audiences; these days, studios only know how to spend too much money in order to lunge after too many eyeballs. (…) Most significantly, TV can react quickly to a changing zeitgeist, whereas movies now take rediculously long to respond to anything, if they even try.'[344]

Quality TV or auteur series follow mostly the dramaturgical rules for epic narrative-performative art and a cinematic aesthetic that pays particular attention to visual dramaturgy and hence moves closer to the tradition of art house cinema or blockbuster productions.

As mentioned already above, the basic structure of classical dramaturgy known from drama has to be combined with the principles of the epic narration and arranged as episodes. A combination of horizontal and vertical dramaturgy gives a series its structure, rhythm, and particular expression. The horizontal dramaturgy is determined by the main character(s) and their occupation, social or family situation. Vertical dramaturgy supports the storyline of the episode or a secondary action also running over a few episodes. Again, the combination of collective and private levels of narration should be applied as well. The following examples are intended to illustrate some of the possible variations in the application of serial dramaturgy that distinguish European and US productions in a significant way, as mentioned above for film productions. The two most important aspects are, summarized in general terms, that in US American productions, the family always forms the core and actions must be psychologically motivated. Family is principally actually the family as a couple with children. Their wellbeing is above all, including the law. Subordinated and as a substitute, a team can be considered a family. In such cases, the members of the family team still hope to have their own family or try to protect their respective children; or they compensate for their loss. In European productions, the freedom of the individual as a member of society stands above the concept of the family as the smallest unit of human existence.

---

344 Lavery 2010, p. 64/66

European Well-Made Series

In recent decades, Scandanavian productions in particular have become successful and and influenced productions made for public broadcasting houses. Amongst others WALLANDER (Mankell S 2005–2013), THE BRIDGE (Rosenfeldt S/Dk 2012–2018), and more. These are often European co-productions, and some of them have been adapted for other channels to better fit them into the cultural and narrative traditions of their region, as WALLANDER or FORBYDELSEN/THE KILLING.

Below, I give a short introduction to particular features of Scandinavian Noir productions. This is followed by a production from Israel, which gave the blueprint to HOMELAND (Gansa & Gordon, USA 2011-), before discussing the fundamental rules for US productions.

FORBYDELSEN [THE KILLING] (Sveistrup 2007–2012)

FORBYDELSEN [THE KILLING] is one of the most famous series within Scandinavian Noir. In this series, the pattern of an analytical drama allows to construct two basic storylines for the horizontal dramaturgy: one focussing on the investigation and the family of the victim, the second reflecting on the politician involved, corruption, and the general condition of society. The third and subordinated but for the aspect of familiarity, necessary narration thread is the individual story of Sarah Lund (Sofie Gråbøl). These three story-lines are interconnected on the level of the horizontal dramaturgy and are braided a fresh for every episode.

The central character is a portrait of a modern, contemporary woman, who appears as a female being, who doesn't have to masquerade as a copy of a male stereotype or unisex detective.

Moreover, which contrary to the stereotypes of most detective series, she is neither lonely nor psychologically shattered. This character is designed as not needing a father figure, caring husband, alcohol or drugs, or extreme sports, to do her job correctly and to ride out the challenges.

The series follows the principles of an analytical drama, when there is first of all the case of the missed/murdered young woman, equivalent to a secret which has to be solved. The main character, Detective Lund, postpones due to her job the dream of starting a new family somewhere in rural Norway. On the individual level, the postponed move to Norway may replace the conflict as in a classic drama construction, since one may hope for an opportunity enabling her to start to start a new family somewhere pleasant and thus reinstall the 'utopian situation'.

When a detective has to solve a crime, there is already a given constellation of good against evil. In modern and entertaining crime series, more than one apparent antagonistic relationship is usually established. In season one, there are corresponding storylines. On the main level, it is the detective-murder constellation. On the other level the detective and the mother of the victim are in opposition. A minor antagonistic situation within the vertical dramaturgy is established between the detective and the politician. Within the horizontal dramaturgy, the series starts with establishing an antagonistic tension between them. The new detective who was going to be the successor to Lund feels that his position is put into question by her staying.

These aspects combined allow a modern dramaturgical approach, using visual narration and reflections on gender stereotypes to add irony to the overall appearance of this series. To give one example, at the beginning, Sarah Lund is packing her things to leave her office. Therefore she takes a picture of her son down from the wall, which her successor replaces a moment later with a poster of revolvers.

The 'collective level', known as one fundamental principle of the dramaturgy of an open form as introduced above, is embedded in the horizontal dramaturgy, hence serving two aspects. The first one is the situation of contemporary society, shaken by corruption, neoliberal politics, misogynistic thinking and paedophilic networks, to name a few. The other is about women who have to assert themselves in patriarchal hierarchies and male-dominated environments. The thread of personal faith is spun over all three storylines: that of the family of the victim, as already mentioned; the private story of Sarah Lund as a single mother working as a professional and a leading investigator in a non-regular and exhausting job; and the private story of the actual politician of every season.[345] The adaptation for the US market changed these aspects substantially.

---

345 cf. Redvall 2013, pp. 159–182; Stutterheim 2015, pp. 362–366

A series that is dramaturgically remarkable, is the Swedish production ARNE DAHL (Diesen, S/D 2011–2015). This production is a very rare
example of a series narrated through an ensemble. This series is an adaptation of a novel series, written by Arne Dahl (Jan Arnald). Opposites that
reflect on the relationship between the individual and society determine the
storylines, the conflict construction and the design of the characters. For
this series, postmodern film aesthetic comes into play. It is referential and
unique at the same time.

As typical for the genre, the dramaturgy is again merging from the
pattern of the analytical drama and a well-made-play. It also has a combination of private and collective threads. On the explicit level, it is a
crime series dealing with the effects of contemporary situations, politics,
and economics. This is reflected in the collective thread of the narration
which results from typical situations effecting the main characters as well
as single events. Although within the narration the characters are situated
in a hierarchical setting – dramaturgically are all the eight characters of
equal importance for the storylines and actions. So they have similar time
lengths of appearance. At first glance, it seems as if a different character
leads every episode. With a closer analysis, it becomes apparent that the
character who appears as leading the single episode gets the most emotional affective private storyline in that episode, but not a more powerful
influence on the intertwined storylines. Since every character leads one
episode to present their story, they remain equals in the horizontal dramaturgy for the season. Thus, gender equality, traditions and stereotypes
about gender and diversity are questioned and contradicted; the irony is
an essential gesture of the design.

After a prelude showing an exemplary and extraordinary incident,
reacting to the theme of urgency within the contemporary zeitgeist, the
ensemble is presented as a team put together for a particular task. They
have to get to know one another alongside the audience to whom they are
introduced. Therefore, no backstory is necessary, no flashbacks, everything
can develop within the progressing narrative. If there is a need for additional
background information, it will be given as resulting from a situation, as
well as by using associative combinations as they happen in everyday life
communication as well. When it makes sense to show characters work
in a duo, the story is structured around pairs. A Persian man who acts

as a cleaner embodies the poetic element,which gives the series moments underscoring the alienation effect - he appears when a member of the team needs some mental or emotional support. When needed – on the explicit level – or appropriate – on the implicit level – this character feeds in a phil-osophical, surreal, fantastic or supporting remark or gesture.

The cinematography (Andréas Lennartsson) provides the balance in the portrait of the contemporary life in Sweden but with an artistic look which gives the series the look of distant but emphatic and knowledge-able observation. The costume design supports individuality and avoids the unisex costumes which are typical for crime-/detective series. The visual dramaturgy altogether challenges traditions and gives the series a unique look.

The dramaturgical concept of the series can be summarised as a conflict between 'children of Enlightenment', modern European citizens, confronted with characters who are driven by criminal energy and a desire for power and influence. The dramatic conflict results from exemplary stories of a con-frontation of open societies with systems primed by coercion and violence. The focus is directed on the ensemble of the detectives. Their professional appearance in relation to their private lives invites empathy; the criminals are kept aesthetically at a distance. As is the tradition of Scandinavian Noir and postmodern aesthetics, the imagined reality is shown in a drastic rep-resentation of violence and its results, using high contrasts and a precise, radical audio-visual approach. 'Murder — that is, in literature thinking, the fundamental conflict with the existing order. The powerful are denied power, the possessing the possession.'[346]

HATUFIM – PRISONERS OF WAR

Another dramaturgically exceptional and most modern narrated series is HATUFIM – PRISONERS OF WAR (Raff ISR 2009–2012). It tells a story re-flecting on the Middle East conflict by condensing it into several intercon-nected storylines.

---

346 Matt 2002, p. 27

The action emerges from a historical incident, which connects two of the earlier mentions 'ideal situations' to start an epic narration, a war-like situation and narrating a biography. Here, it is an ensemble of characters. Their diverse biographies, as told in the series, are influenced by actual events and and related to one another within contemporary society. So not only their traits can be given a complex expression but also situation of society becomes manifest.

Seventeen years after they were captured, politicians agree that the Red Cross will bring three prisoners of war home, one of them presumed dead. Three families are going to have the missing son/husband/fiancé back. How to resettle after such a long time of having been imprisoned, tortured, excluded from any social life? The three families are situated in the three distinct cities Tel Aviv, Jerusalem and Haifa. Accordingly, they represent different habits, traditions and world views. Thus, the series gives an exemplary cross-section of contemporary Israel. The narration is arranged as poly-perspective. The conflict like situation arises here from the encounter of those who were imprisoned and away for such a long time with their families, close ones, friends, and representatives of the state Israel. That way female and male experiences are placed in dialogue, as well as the perspective of different generations. In this series, the female characters are the dramaturgically central characters starting the action before it becomes an equal and dialogic arranged poly-perspective narrative. Two officers of the secret service are situated in the centre, as representatives different approaches to their job and life. These are versions of the Central Self, asking questions, observing and commenting on events, thus giving a reflection and context to the story unfolding.

The series is reminiscent of LIFE ACCORDING TO AGFA (Dayan, ISR 1993). Although, in HATUFIM, the situation developed over decades, but the central conflict still impinges upon the lives of very many people. Universal, as well as exceptional in this narrative, is the situation of someone coming home from war and being traumatised. At the horizontal, explicit level it is told how the characters involved deal with an extreme situation, challenging everyone involved. These are fragmented into episodes which give a closer look into the individual stories. Implicit themes of universal interest are embedded in the narrative. The series is dealing with 'basic possibilities of human socialisation', like marriage and death.[347] The motif of marriage can be understood as reconciliation with the world and the circumstances, as 'comprehensive reconciliation with the general order'.[348] In HATUFIM the motif of the wedding conflicts with cruel forms of death, torture and murder. This tension determines the action as well as the interaction of the characters in this series.[349]

The Contemporary US Success Model(s)

In principle, all fundamental rules are valid for US productions in the same way as introduced above. The difference is minimal but of importance. For US Series it's of no relevance whether its produced for a public broadcaster, a pay channel or an online distributor, the specifics of 'American dramaturgy'[350] must be taken into account. Here, only a summary of the distinctiveness of 'American Dramaturgy' will be presented:

What all the US productions have in common is that they focus on family issues. Either as a family whose future must be guaranteed (BREAKING BAD (Gilligan USA 2008–2013)); the team as a family of characters, THE WIRE (Simon USA 2002–2008), CSI, whose central character has lost his family in dramatic circumstances, while the other characters hope to establish one, NCIS, and THE MENTALIST (Heller USA 2008–2015). Or, these aspects combined as in BONES (Hanson USA 2005–2017). Alternatively, the family involving business or business-like activities provides the framework: DYNASTY, SOPRANOS, THE MARVELOUS MRS. MEISEL (Sherman-Palladino USA 2017-), a variation of this is a family on a farm: BONANZA, LITTLE HOUSE ON THE PRAIRIE.

NCIS

NCIS (Bellisario & McGill, 2003-) is one of the most often watched and longest running prime time TV series in the United States and sold

---

347 Matt 2002, p. 27
348 Matt 2002, p. 27
349 Cf. Stutterheim 2015, pp. 366/367
350 Cf. Belton 2009; Fiedler 2017; Gelfert 2006; Stutterheim 2015, p. 153–160

worldwide. The horizontal dramaturgy is arranged around the head of a unit, going with the name of Leroy Jethro Gibbs (Mark Harmon). His character is a centre figure as introduced above. Gibbs can be understood as a modern variant of a Western sheriff. This central character lives for the law, although his private life suffers from it. This principle also applies to the central figures of the spin-offs NCIS: New Orleans and NCIS: Los Angeles. The equivalent to Gibbs in the L.A. spin off is established as a Supervisory Special Agent, Henriette 'Hetty' Lange (Linda Hunt), introduced as the team's Operational Manager. For the dramaturgical lead of the horizontal dramaturgy, her character is linked with that of a male member of the team. The audience's emotional attention is drawn to the male special agent G. Callen (Chris O'Donnell), who has been provided with an extraordinary background story for this. Thus, for every episode one of these two characters can be of substantial influence on the action while the other continues in the background. This principle helps to make the entire horizontal narrative varied, but also to tell the respective episodes in an enthralling way.

On the explicit level, the members of a team of each of the NCIS versions form a group of investigators who work together. To organise the story lines, they are arranged in pairs.

With the established ensemble as a team of characters with different talents and biographies, it is possible to weave in one or more subplots, in which one or more private aspects of team members can be narrated, in addition to the central vertical action of the particular episode. On the implicit level, on the collective thread, the leading characters represent the Navy. This institution is represented as the refuge of the good, a community, and the characters are proud to belong to it. This background for the action and development of the strands of action implies the consent of civil society with its ethics and politics, as well as the promise of guarantee for the protection or preservation of national security and norms. Since each spin-off series is located in a different part and jurisdiction within the United States, it is possible to customize the team and dramaturgical structure for each unique version.

The family-like unity is a core element for most of the television series produced in the USA, for the American market. Therefore, the cast ranges in age and covers two or three generations of both genders. On the horizontal

Fig. 46: © Jasper Stutterheim

level, the members of the ensemble bring in just as much private life to keep the audience interested in the long run of the series. To give the extended story hold, all main characters are shown to come back to the one place, the headquarter. The range of embodiments of fictional characters offers different members of the audience to choose with whom they might feel close or identify with. Alternatively, as is often the case with such series, to see them as part of one's own family.

GAME OF THRONES

In recent years the term 'Game-of-Thrones-Dramaturgy' has been used time and again. The series reached a vast audience worldwide. Hence, this sub-chapter attempts to give a first overview of the noticeable features of the dramaturgy of the series. Although the final disappointed many of their audience, this series was of substantial influence to TV productions made in the 2010s.[351]

GAME OF THRONES (Benioff & Weiss, USA 2011–2019) is epic and multi-perspective narrated. Benioff and Weiss deal with topics as mentioned above: power, war, violence, trust and betrayal, love and marriage, death and murder. The series runs over eight seasons, altogether 86 episodes, produced by HBO, and broadcasted between 2011 and 2019. It is one of the most complex constructions for a series as far as I am informed. It spans 86 episodes, about hundred hours of an extensive constructed and sophisticated woven epic narration.

For this series, the horizontal dramaturgy is a linear-causal structure, epic and arranged in episodes and scenes. Intertwining between four and seven storylines within an episode is an unique feature of this series. All of these narrative threats are related to each other and parallel arranged. Such a broad group of different characters as arranged in this production allows attracting a broad audience since these many individuals enable various forms of identification.

As it is commonly known, the first season of a series for American television must always be written, directed, and produced in such a way that it is possible to either stop or continue the story after season one. With the extraordinary success of the first season of GAME OF THRONES, it was foreseeable that the series would continue and produced until the end is told.

---

351 More detailed dramaturgical analysis on GAME OF THRONES is published in (Stutterheim 2017) and for season eight in blog posts at www.kino-glaz.de

For the series, the authors have adapted R.R. Martin's novels to the requirements of cinematic narration. The narrative is spread over several levels but bond by the ultimate meaning. In comparison to the novels, which are written from the author's evaluative and descriptive perspective, the series tells poly-perspectival. Changing this made it possible to switch to a modern dramaturgy. By adapting, Benioff and Weiss also changed the rhythm of the narration.

On the implicit level, the story is a metaphor about power and the question who rules or should rule the world. The series tells the old, universal story of good versus evil. Implicit, it represents the moral of traditional Christian world views as inherited in the US cultural memory. The concept of the biological family as the nucleus of all human relationships is again core for the overall plot.

The horizontal dramaturgy of the series is, from a dramaturgical point of view, got arranged as a very long movie. Therefore, one can detect that the series as such is arranged following the principles of a five-act-drama. A chain of events initiates the action. As Hegel writes, a war is one of the 'ideal' situations from which an epic narrative is created. Such an extreme circumstance reveals the true character of a nation and also that of individuals.[352] A protagonist can be established who represents a principle and is the center figure of a group respective an ensemble. Thus, their role is to personify core aspects of the theme the series represents. As typical for the dramaturgical pattern of a dramatic narration of a dramatic epos, their character is introduced as the one who reacts to the circumstances in the first part of the series. After the moment of anagnorisis and peripeteia, this character is positioned and developed as the person able to acting more decisively, given the situation which he had not caused himself and which has been fuelled by war and catastrophe. This male protagonist is mirrored by a female character with whom he is connected by a situation known from theatre tradition. By handing over a special gift followed by body contact, the bounding of these two characters is sealed. So one of them can lead a part of the action and implied the other is always involved. That allows arranging the storyline

---

352 Hegel 2003, p. 134

more flexible, attractive and enriched with moments of surprise. Some of the characters represent definite principles, and others are designed more flexible. They created an ensemble of primary and secondary characters in which one can embed particular principles. In addition, they introduced characters like Theon Greyjoy (Allen Alfie) and Jaime Lannister (Nikolaj Coster-Waldau), which can be moved more flexible for almost the whole series. Thus the dramaturgical principles are less evident to the audience. Nevertheless, in the end, in season 8, these characters act accordingly principles of the 'American Dramaturgy': they try to secure their family and are punished for their sins.

In this series an array of characters arranged who represent the evil, which one can interpret as versions of Shakespeare's *Richard III* crossed over with *Macbeth*. This relay race of evil characters starts with Joffrey Baratheon (Jack Gleeson), to Walder Frey (David Bradley), for a short time also Theon Greyjoy joins this principle before he is replaced by Ramsey Bolton (Iwan Rheon), who hands over to the next. Running parallel, the character of Little Finger (Aidan Gillen) steps in for additional episodic moments representing evil, betray, meanness. All these characters are human versions of the evil south of the wall, not to forget the character of Jaqen H'gar (Tom Wlashiha), who represents the fascist version of the novel, representing the ultimate No-One.[353] On the ultimate good-evil dimension it is the Night King (Richard Brake; Vladimir Furdik) as ultimate Evil who is overturned by Arya (Maisie Williams) - or the character who is going to be the new King of the Kingdoms - in the catastrophe, the Showdown, in the final season. This Night King character is directly bound to Bran Stark through touch and spiritual connection. The evil is not eliminated with the death of Satan, it manifests in the end in Daenerys (Emilia Clarke), and stays alive when the new king and his council are not the 'good good people'[354] but result from betrayal.

The whole action is organised as heading towards a catastrophe and catharsis. Overall, it is obvious that the dramaturgical concept is orientated

---

353 Arendt 2010, 87/88, Stutterheim 2017, p. 87/88
354 Gelfert, p. 46–50

on that of Shakespeare's History Plays, merging the *Bible* and the legend of the Holy Grail into one new fantastic epos. The creators and author-directors of this series adopt and merge dramaturgical traditions knowns from theatre and cinema. They orientate themselves also towards Anton Chekhov, Andreij Tarkovsky, Fritz Lang, Akiro Kurosava, and William Friedkin, amongst others.[355]

The Chronotopos of GAME OF THRONES represents an 'unspecific past'[356] resembling the time of the Middle Ages in the history of the British Isles. The narrated time is arranged most of the time chronologically proceeding. Only a few retrospectives happen and are embedded in the narrative arranged as a 'shining' of one of the seers, most often as Bran's visions. Space grows from two antagonistic areas in the beginning and enlarges constantly and immeasurable. The topography is as fantastic as the story and hence not to contextualise with our contemporary knowledge about the geography of the British Isles or planet Earth. The topography as well resembles maps and assumptions about continents from sometime around or before the Middle Ages. Due to the association of an unspecific past in combination with fantasy, also the topography becomes believable. In GAME OF THRONES a symbolic thing, the 'Iron Throne', demonstrates the point of convergence, and as the physical representation of the ultimate power.

The storyline is arranged along one central conflict, the aim to crown a new king/queen able to heal the country and bring peace, which is interconnected with the spiritual/implicit conflict of good against evil, humanity against death and destruction, as well as civilisation versus life in the Wild West respective Wild North in this case. Every season gets several sub-conflicts, one storyline per season is composed as an intrigue led by Cersei, every season a different one. Each of the main characters gets a particular storyline, shorter or longer levels of narration that are parallel but interconnected by the central conflict.

Music and sound design contribute to the overall aesthetic concept. Not just the title music is reminiscent of a traditional wedding waltz, beginning with one couple, which invites the next to join the dance and so on until

---

355 Benioff and Weiss USA 2016, Bonus Material, First Season, Disk one
356 for the term of an 'unspecific past' cf. Varga 1991, 148/149

as many as possible couples are dancing. However, it is not a classic waltz, here is a beat/note missing and Djawadi's composition for the title sequence gives the impression of an open form, of a surprise in the familiar. Djawadi also composed Leitmotifs and themes for every house, the main characters, and for some of the places.

The very first episode begins with a prelude, introducing the antagonistic constellation of the human beings and evil creatures as well as the existence of two areas representing these antagonistic powers, separated by an exceptional and fantastic wall. This short episode is already highly artificial, postmodern referential. This sequence introduces the good-evil metaphor, the genre convention as a crossover of fantasy and horror, but already contains an ironic approach. In particular, the visual style and its referentiality establishes a form of alienation-effect.[357] As mentioned above already, one element of importance for the unique aesthetic of the series is its theatricality. With the opening sequence, theatre gets referenced to when the iron curtain has to be lifted first before the action can begin. Other than typical in contemporary film editing, it is shown how figures enter and exit a room or place. Speeches get given from stage-like rostras as performances given to an audience, to mention some aspects of theatricality here.

Jon Snow (Kit Harrington) gets established as the protagonist. He is introduced in the first scene after the titles. Here, the figure speaks the first sentence of the main action, when he supports his younger brother, Bran (Isaac Hempstead-Wright), as it appears in that situation. A moment later the attraction of the audience is directed onto the figure of the patriarch, Eddard/Ned Stark (Sean Bean). From tradition as well as by the dramaturgical design of the exposition, the active input onto the developing story comes for some episodes from the character of Ned Stark. The principle of Winterfell gets represented by both characters, the father and the Bastard. Jon Snow is the outcast of the Winterfell-family-level and equipped with a secret. This Stark-family is established as representatives of the good people, who are respecting the law, tradition and duty, a great and loving family like the Cartwright's in BONANZA (Dortort, USA 1959–1973) or the Ingall's

---

357 Stutterheim 2017, pp. 12–18

from the LITTLE HOUSE ON THE PRAIRIE. The Starks are a typical family of the Western genre, living at the border to a dangerous territory where the `wild people' use to live.

In season one, the character introduced as Jon gets several opportunities to establish his position as being on eye level to the Ned Stark character and moreover to represent the same principles as the patriarch does. In episode I-1, in the scene in which they find the 'Dire Wolfs', it becomes apparent. In this situation is Jon only character who is shown on eye level to Eddard Stark, who is introduced to be his father - visually and argumentative. In this tense situation, Jon is not only allowed to object to Ned Stark's decision but as well to convince him to revise his decision. That Jon Snow is not only reasonable but also unselfish when he saves the lives of these innocent wolf babies increases his appearance as a good person. Resulting from this situation, it becomes probable and believable that the character of Jon Snow can take over the lead from the character of Eddard Stark at the end of the establishing season, which functions as an equivalent to an exposition of a movie. Antagonistic to them introduced are the Lannisters, who appear like a cliché of the French. They are situated in the sunny and summery Kings Landing, resembling London though. They are in power of the 'White House' of this series, the palace of the king over the kingdoms. Independently, they are one of the wealthy and strong royal families, ruling one of the seven kingdoms. In GAME OF THRONES, the Kingdom is a Super-Kingdom, as the United Kingdom or the United States of America, combining seven Kingdoms, as the seven brothers of the Grimm's tale *The Seven Ravens*. A family, their 'house represent each of these kingdoms,' a phrase that gives them a character trail, and an iconic sign. Each of these houses gets its narrative thread, their ensemble and a center figure, as well as a colour design and a musical leitmotif. Although these narrative levels are situated in different places or areas, and some figures might never meet each other in the narrated story. These different levels are arranged as dramaturgically interacting. The incident causing the action, results from a sin and its discovery – the incest[358] of the characters of Cersei Lannister (Lena Heday) and her brother Jamie

---

358 Cf. Leveticus and Deuteronomy in the Old Testament/Torah

(Nikolaj Coster-Waldau). This beginning can also be read as a reference to the legend of the Holy Grail, again, in particular the aspect of the country suffering when and as long as the king is sick[359] (any kind of illness, mental or physical) – or as it is extended here, missing. It can only be cured by Parzival, the knight who was hidden from the world of the crown, far away, in the woods. When his time comes, he has to learn the rules and language and skills of the knights and nobles. In this plot, Jon Snow (Kit Harrington) is hidden in Winterfell who becomes the hero who has to learn the rules of a region and status alien to him and it is he who has to save the world of the good ones, the kingdom. As a mirrored version to the Parzival-constellation introduced above, Jon's character becomes the spiritual knight and gets supported by the knight Arya, who resembles Gaiwan, and therefore she has to be the one who defeats the Night King.

In season six, when it gets revealed that Jon is a descendant of the royal family, the aim of the character is set, and a new internal conflict established that will keep the audience attracted until the end. Will Jon/Eagon become the new king or Daenerys? Very soon many hints and dramaturgical tradition point towards Daenerys' metamorphosis into the evil incarnation of a dictator. Many explicit as well as implicit aspects, suggest that Jon/Eagon might be the only one able to rescue the Kingdom, the people and secure peace. His character would bring north and south, city and country together as well as families. He inherits traditions of both antagonistic parts of the Seven Kingdoms; he is the reborn chosen by the new God who in turn helped to defeat the army of Satan.

Another character to be mentioned here is Tyron (Peter Dinklage) who gets, as one of the few who could do so, sent across most of the territories and storylines. He is the outcast of his family and also a representation of the central self for the whole series. This Tyrion is commenting on many events, explaining context and background, and by understanding and discussing the philosophical context, he also explains the behaviour of one or the other figure during action - for the audience.

The authors arrange antagonistic pairs, which gives the episodes a dramatic structure, an internal conflict, suspense and closure. Substantial good-evil constructions bring about a stable net of familiar oppositions.

---

359 Eschenbach 1994

By composing some characters as complex and not easy to judge, who are changed throughout the action, the moment of surprise is guaranteed. Some of these are not fixed and are floating. Such characters are Theon Greyjoy, the Hound (Rory McCann), and Jamie Lannister.

Moments of catastrophe and catharsis are arranged over alternate episodes. The first conflict to be solved is spiritual, that between good and evil, the humans and their god versus Satan. After it is achieved that the human world will continue to exist, worldly matters must be solved. Another battle fought, the human world is shattered as well. In the end, a new king must be appointed. However, no new royal family is created, only an interim king is appointed.

Although, this series seems to be an exceptionally complex and new state of the art of a series, with a close look one can detect the traditional pattern arranged in a new costume, except the end of this particular production.

The main aim for which the characters fight for is the integrity of their families which need a functioning state or realm, that provides basic rules of coexistence allowing independence of each family. That is the conceptual frame known from series like BREAKING BAD,[360] NCIS or BONES and many more. 'Family first, America first.' The biological family is the nucleus. The incident triggering the action results from bad and egoistic behaviour that endangers the principle of 'family first' and consequently, the principles of coexistence within the nation. The action gets led by male characters, which are supplemented by female characters. As it is typical for a Western, the outlaws have to prove themselves as good people. As a result, as an element of the catharsis, most of them but the one which – from a dramaturgical point of view was established over 85 out of 86 episodes as the character who consequently must become the new king – get the chance to start a new life from a privileged position.

After nine years of complex and well-told stories, with characters that have impressed and captivated the audience, the series ends with sequences of illogical events that lead to an uninspired and no longer complex and interestingly told stoppage.

The first 30 minutes of the final episode were a consistent and likely continuation of the previous episode. The figure of Tyrion (Peter Dinklage) sets off in search of his siblings and is shocked by their death. Jon-Aegon

(Kit Harrington) tries to prevent last mad acts in the destroyed city, but he did not succeed because he does not reveal his true identity. The figure of Grey Worm (Jacob Anderson), on the other hand, has blindly adopted his queen's madness and one of those who has given up his identity carries out her orders mercilessly as a No-One.

Daenerys (Emilia Clarke) continues to show her true character traits as a fascist commander who calls for a 'total war'. Where do the many Unsullied and Dothraki fighters suddenly come from in such flocks, after being considerably decimated in both previous battles?

The figure of the Tyrion gets a little honour back when he dares to quit as the hand of the queen. Arrested and incarcerated, he is able to convince Jon-Aegon that the only rescue - for himself and Westeros - can come from him. His duty is to keep Daenerys from further mad deeds that would also hit him, Jon, and his sisters. Jon-Aegon stabs the mass murderer, amasingly still beloved by him. The fact that the dragon child notices this immediately and approaches it also lies just in the logic of the previous narrative. Also, that he does not murder Jon-Aegon, but makes the throne melting away, can be believed just so, resulting from the logic of the previous narrative. But then we experience a radical change in the quality of the dramaturgy, like the narrative.

From this moment on, illogical sequences of events meet a persiflage of the previous series.

How does Grey Worm (Jacob Andersen) and everyone else knew that Jon-Aegon had stabbed Daenerys. There was nobody there, and the dragon flew with her into the far distance before anyone could see her being murdered with their own eyes. Did Jon tell everyone what he did? Why should he? So, how does Jon get into the dungeon, and why without objection of any of the others from those characters still alive? Got Grey Worm so powerful that no one could stand up to him and stop him from threatening Jon with the death penalty? Unlikely, in the sense of the story as it got told so far. Has Arya suddenly lost all her abilities or for whatever reason has given up her trust and hopes in the brother who is now a cousin? The Arya as developed for the episodes before would have been able to free him, for example.

Then, when it comes to appointing the new king, everyone, including Sam (John Bradley) and Bran (Isaak Hempstead Wright), have forgotten that Jon would be the rightful heir to the throne, although until a few minutes earlier everyone still assumed that he should be the one and only king of Westeros. They did everything in their power to make him and others aware of this fact. What happened to them? Do they resent his love for Daenerys? But how can this be a reason? Jon separated himself from her in the most drastic way imaginable. This ending presented in the last hour of the series is therefore also illogical, in the sense of the previous action. Even Tyrion has forgotten that a moment ago Jon/Aegon saved his life. The dragon would have cremated him by now, and now he suggests Bran be the new king and Jon to stay prisoner, why? Because of the knowledge that Bran gathered through his spiritual abilities? If so, Sam could have been king there too.

Who quickly rebuilt the hall that had just been destroyed and who repaired the chairs in no time in which the king's advisers now sit together? It is entirely absurd, dramaturgically seen, that Jon returns to Castle Black, and welcomed there by Tormund Giantsbane (Kristofer Hivju) and then Jon rides further north with his old buddy, fishing and hunting? To enjoy life as buddies?

The decision concerning the figure of Arya can be interpreted as to be and consistent because she got developed into a person who does not fit into the moral concept of this Westeros Arya behaves against the rules and carries the only blink of a reflection of feminism within the series. To move on corresponds to the activities of this character as they were shown in the course of the action. In this sense, her journey beyond the borders known so far represents a consequent end when Westeros is given into the hands of an asexual spiritual leader who is balanced with men who are devoted to alcohol and enjoying to spend time with prostitutes.

So much narrative effort, involving gods, Satan, choice, secrets, family ties. However, in the end, we must listen to a discussion about the reconstruction of brothels; and that Jon is changed and not presented accepting to be Aegon after all. Although he did so a few episodes back in the family crypt. But, in his heartache, he suddenly mutated into a character who doesn't care about anybody else? So many lives/characters sacrificed to get him, the chosen one, at the throne, and then he gets shown to have decided for fishing.

From a dramaturgical point of view, this end has little to do with the plot told for over 85 hours or more. An ingenious and surprising postmodern twist on declaring everything to be the author's dream or imagination this end does not offer either, although the series has operated to some extent with the aesthetics of postmodern cinema. Also in postmodern movies, there must be a logic in presenting such a twist, which gets prepared long before it happens, due to the fundamental rules of dramaturgy for film and audio-visual time-based narrations.

A good ending is crucial. In film dramaturgy, everything is composed to drive towards the ending; and to achieve this requires a well-woven story, that is within the framework of the conventions one set for the plot as logical as possible and presenting a probably evolving progressive chain of events. In a film, unlike to a novel, the ending must be a consequence resulting from the course of the plot. The rules of the literary narrative are a little different from those of film drama, which has its roots in theatre and performing narrative. A cinematic narrative is bound to a time-space continuum, it is perceived by the audience at the moment. The film is 'time-based', therefore the dramaturgy for an observing audience must be organised in such a way that the events result in an interplay of family structures and surprising twists and turns or a surprising arrangement, as well as a logical and probable development within the framework of the cosmos, presented and its rules. The crux here is that the last hour of this series does not correspond to the conventions of the imagined cosmos in which the action takes place; and thus is not in the least logical and probably a result of the action. This disappoints the really large fan-audience as well as the few academics, who have followed this series with interest. This also reduces the chance for a successful sequel, as the disappointed fans will now hardly hope for a continuation.

While the 'Game-of-Thrones-Dramaturgy' has so far been spoken of with admiration, this final episode has also destroyed this enthusiasm for many.

Postscript

The different forms – minor and core – known in modern dramaturgy can be adapted individually by combining fundamental concepts with variable elements in order to support the story. The decisions made at the level of the explicit dramaturgy (structure, characters, form, chronology and more) are always supported by elements of the implicit level of dramaturgy. This level has to be arranged for every story a new. As writer/director and creative team, one can orientate oneself according to the parameter introduced in earlier chapters. Nevertheless, every plot requires a particular aesthetic design that supports the story to be told and the theme embedded in it.

Table of Figures

Bibliography

Abeel, E. (2014). Looking For Love Over Nicotine and Caffeine; Jim Jarmusch Talks About "Coffee and Cigarettes". Retrieved 10 Aug 2018 https://www.indiewire.com/2004/05/looking-for-love-over-nicotine-and-caffeine-jim-jarmusch-talks-about-coffee-and-cigarettes-78919/

Adorno, T. W. (2003). *Philosophie der neuen Musik* Frankfurt am Main suhrkamp

Adorno, T. W. (2010). *Einführung in die Dialektik (1958)* Frankfurt am Main: Suhrkamp.

Alter, R. (2011). *The art of biblical narrative* (Rev. & updated ed.). New York: Basic Books.

Almodóvar, P. (E 2004) LA MALA EDUCACIÓN.

Anderson, M. (1962). Das Wesen der Tragödie. In H. Frenz (Ed.), *Amerikanische Dramaturgie* (pp. 28–35). Reinbek bei Hamburg: Rowohlt Verlag.

Antonioni, M. (I/F 1961). LA NOTTE.

Arendt, Hannah. 2010. *Über das Böse. Eine Vorlesung zu Fragen der Ethik*. Translated by Ursula Ludz. München: Piper Verlag.

Aristoteles, & Schmitt, A. (Eds.). (2008). *Aristoteles: Poetik. Übersetzt und erläutert von Arbogast Schmitt*. Berlin: Akademie-Verlag.

Aristotle, & Lucas, D. W. (1968). *Poetics. Introduction, commentary and appendixes by D. W. Lucas*. Oxford: Clarendon Press.

Arnold, J. (2001). *Inquisition and power: catharism and the confessing subject in medieval Languedoc*. Philadelphia: University of Pennsylvania Press.

Aronofski, D. (USA 2010). BLACK SWAN.

Assmann, A. (2010). *Memory in a global age: discourses, practices and trajectories* (1. publ. ed.). Basingstoke: Palgrave Macmillan.

Assmann, A. (2011). *Cultural memory and Western civilization: functions, media, archives*. New York: Cambridge University Press.

Assmann, J. (2002). *Das kulturelle Gedächtnis: Schrift, Erinnerung und politische Identität in frühen Hochkulturen.* München: Beck.

Assmann, J. (2004). *Religion und kulturelles Gedächtnis: zehn Studien* (2. Aufl. ed.). München: Beck.

Assmann, J. (2006). *Religion and cultural memory: ten studies.* Stanford, Calif.: Stanford Univ. Press.

Assmann, J. (2007). *Das kulturelle Gedächtnis: Schrift, Erinnerung und politische Identität in frühen Hochkulturen* (6. ed.). München: Beck.

Assmann, J. (2011). *Cultural memory and early civilization: writing, remembrance, and political imagination.* Cambridge; New York: Cambridge University Press.

Bachtin, M. M. (1979). *Die Ästhetik des Wortes* (R. G. Grübel, Trans. Erstausg ed.). Frankfurt am Main: Suhrkamp.

Bachtin, M. M. (1986). *Untersuchungen zur Poetik und Theorie des Romans.* Berlin und Weimar: Aufbau-Verlag.

Bachtin, M. M. (2008a). *Autor und Held in der ästhetischen Tätigkeit.* Frankfurt am Main: Suhrkamp.

Bachtin, M. M. (2008b). *Chronotopos.* Frankfurt am Main: Suhrkamp.

Bachtin, M. M. (2011). *Zur Philosophie der Handlung.* Berlin: Matthes & Seitz.

Bailey, Terry. 2014. "Normatizing the silent drama: Photoplay manuals of the 1910s and early 1920s." *Journal of Screenwriting. Intellect. 5* (2):209–224. doi: 10.1386/josc.5.2.209_1.

Balázs, B. (2001). *Der Geist des Films.* Frankfurt am Main: Suhrkamp.

Ball, L. (USA 1951–1957). I LOVE LUCY.

Bazin, A. (2004). *What is cinema?.* Berkeley: University of California Press.

Bazin, A., Bitomsky, H., & Truffaut, F. (1975). *Was ist Kino?: Bausteine zur Theorie des Films.* Köln: DuMont Schauberg.

Becker, A. (2004). *Perspektiven einer anderen Natur zur Geschichte und Theorie der filmischen Zeitraffung und Zeitdehnung.* Bielefeld: transcript.

Bellisario, D. P., & McGill, D. (2003-). *NCIS: Naval Criminal Investigative Service.*

Belton, J. (2009). *American cinema/American culture* (3 ed.). New York, NY: McGraw-Hill.

Benioff, D., & Weiss, D. B. (USA 2011–2019). GAME OF THRONES. HBO.

Benjamin, W. (1977). Was ist das epische Theater (1) - Versuche ueber Brecht. In H. Schweppenhäuser & R. Tiedemann (Eds.), *Walter Benjamin - Gesammelte Werke* (Vol. II-2 Aufsaetze, Essays, Vortraege, pp. 519–531). Frankfurt am Main: Suhrkamp Taschenbuch Wissenschaft.

Benjamin, W. (1991a). Ursprung des deutschen Trauerspiels (1928). In H. Schweppenhaeuser (Ed.), *Gesammelte Schriften / Walter Benjamin* (Vol. I-1, pp. 203–430). Frankfurt am Main: suhrkamp.

Benjamin, W. (2011). Ursprung des deutschen Trauerspiels (1928). In: P. Langemeyer (Ed.), *Dramentheorie: Texte vom Barock bis zur Gegenwart* (pp. 416–428). Stuttgart: Reclam.

Bentley, E., & Hasenclever, W. (1967). *Das lebendige Drama: Eine elementare Dramaturgie*. Velber bei Hannover: Friedrich Verlag.

Bergman, I. (S 1957). DET SJUNDE INSEGLET [The Seventh Seal].

Bergman, I. (S 1968). VARGTIMMEN - [The Hour of the Wolf].

Besson, L. (F 1997). THE FIFTH ELEMENT.

Bickerton, E. (2009). *A short history of Cahiers du cinéma*. London; New York: Verso.

Biener, K. (1990). *Henrik Ibsen und das Pièce Bien Fait*. (Diplom), Humboldt-Universität Berlin.

Blavatsky, H. P. (1960). *Isis unveiled: a master key to the mysteries of ancient and modern science and theology* (Vol. 1: The 'Infallibility' of Modern Science). Pasadena, Calif.: Theosophical University Press.

Blažević, M. (2016). Complex in-betweenness of Dramaturgy. In: M. Romanska (Ed.), *The Routledge Companien to Dramaturgy* (pp. 329–334). Oxon, New York: Routledge.

Blothner, D. (1999). *Erlebniswelt Kino: Über die unbewußte Wirkung des Films*. Bergisch Gladbach: Bastei-Verl. Lübbe.

Booth, W. C. (1983). *The rhetoric of fiction* (2nd ed.). Harmondsworth: Penguin, 1987.

Bordwell, D. (2006). *The way Hollywood tells it: Story and style in modern movies*. Berkeley [u.a.]: Univ. of California Press.

Bordwell, D., Staiger, J., & Thompson, K. (Eds.). (2006). *The classical Hollywood cinema: Film style and mode of production to 1960* (Repr. ed.). London: Routledge.

Braulich, H. (1983). Max Reinhardts theatralische Vision von Mensch und Raum. In M. Kuschnia (Ed.), *100 Jahre Deutsches Theater Berlin 1883–1983* (pp. 66–69). Berlin: Henschel Verlag.

Brecht, B. (1948). Kleines Organon für das Theater. In S. Verlag & E. Hauptmann (Eds.), *Bertolt Brecht Gesammelte Werke - Schriften zum Theater 2* (Vol. 16, pp. 661–707). Frankfurt am Main: Suhrkamp Verlag.

Brecht, B. (1966a). Dialoge aus dem Messingknauf. In *Über Theater* (pp. 22–126). Leipzig: Philipp Reclam jun.

Brecht, B. (1966b). Die dialektische Dramatik (1931). In *Über Theater* (pp. 6–20). Leipig: Philipp Reclam jun.

Brecht, B. (1966c). Episches Theater. In *Über Theater* (pp. 311/312). Leipzig: Philipp Reclam jun.

Brecht, B. (1966d). Episches Theater. In *Über Theater* (pp. 344). Leipzig: Philipp Reclam jun.

Brecht, B. (1966e). [episches und dialektisches theater]. In *Über Theater* (pp. 350–352). Leipzig: Verlag Philipp Reclam jun.

Brecht, B. (1966f). Kleines Organon für das Theater (1948). In W. Hecht (Ed.), *Über Theater* (pp. 205–243). Leipzig: Verlag Philipp Reclam jun. Leipzig.

Brecht, B. (1967). *Gesammelte Werke 15. Schriften zum Theater 1* (113.-124. Tsd.: 1977 ed.). Frankfurt am Main: Suhrkamp.

Brecht, B. (1977). Über den Beruf des Schauspielers. In *Gesammelte Werke* (Vol. 15: Schriften zum Theater 1, pp. 391–436).

Brook, P., Carrière, J.-C., & Lubtchansky, W. (2007). *The Mahabharata*. London: British Film Institute.

Brooker, Charlie. (USA 2011-). BLACK MIRROR.

Büchner, G., Weidig, L., & Enzensberger, H. M. (1974). *Der Hessische Landbote Texte, Briefe, Prozessakten*. Frankfurt a. M.: Insel.

Burdorf, D., Fasbender, C., Moennighoff, B., Schweikle, G., & Schweikle, I. (2007). *Metzler Lexikon Literatur: Begriffe und Definitionen*. Stuttgart: Metzler.

Bürger, G. A., & Raspe, R. E. (1968). *Munchausen. Wunderbare Reisen zu Wasser und zu Lande*. Frankfurt am Main: Insel Verlag.

Burt, G. (1994). *The art of film music: special emphasis on Hugo Friedhofer, Alex North, David Raksin, Leonard Rosenman*. Boston: Northeastern University Press.

Burton, R. F. S., Finamore, R., & Lopez, A. (1985). *Tales from the thousand and one nights*. New York: Stewart, Tabori & Chang.

Carlson, M. A. (1984). *Theories of the theatre: a historical and critical survey from the Greeks to the present*. Ithaca, N.Y.: Cornell University Press.

Carné, M. (F 1945). LES ENFANTS DU PARADIS.

Carrière, J.-C. (1994). *The secret language of film*. New York: Pantheon Books.

Carrière, J.-C. (1999). *Über das Geschichtenerzählen*. Berlin: Alexander-Verl.

Carrière, J.-C. (2003). *Der unsichtbare Film*. Berlin: Alexander-Verl.

Carrière, J.-C., & Bonitzer, P. (1999). *Praxis des Drehbuchschreibens*. Berlin: Alexander-Verl.

Carter, C. (USA 1996–1999). MILLENNIUM.

Cervantes Saavedra, M. d. (1810). *Don Quichotte de la Manche*. Paris: Briand.

Cimino, M. (USA 1978). THE DEER HUNTER.

Cocteau, J. (F 1946). LA BELLE ET LA BÊTE.

Coelsch-Foisner, S. (2005). Preface: The Author as Reader -- Textual Visions and Revisions. In *The Author as Reader* (pp. vii–xi). Salzburg: Peter Lang Publishing.

Cohan, S., & Hark, I. R. (1997). *The road movie book*. London; New York: Routledge.

Comolli, J.-L. *Cinema against spectacle: Technique and ideology revisited*.

Cuarón, A. (UK/USA 2013). GRAVITY.

Daldry, S. (USA/UK 2002). THE HOURS.

Dammbeck, L. (D 2003). DAS NETZ.

Dancyger, K., & Rush, J. (2013). *Alternative scriptwriting: beyond the Hollywood formula*. Burlington, MA; Abingdon, Oxon: Focal Press.

Danko, K. (2005). Tennessee Williams's Textual Visions and Revisions. In S. Coelsch-Foisner (Ed.), *The Author as Reader* (pp. 215–234). Salzburg: Peter Lang Publishing.

Daxelmüller, C. (1996). *Aberglaube, Hexenzauber, Höllenängste eine Geschichte der Magie*. München: Dt. Taschenbuch-Verl.

Dayan, A. (ISR 1993). LIFE ACCORDING TO AGFA [OT: אפגא יפ לע מייחה].

De Palma, B. (USA/CAN 2007). REDACTED.

Despoix, P. (2003). Ironisch/Ironie. In K. Barck (Ed.), *Ästhetische Grundbegriffe* (pp. 196–244). Stuttgart; Weimar: Verlag J.B. Metzler.

Diesen, H. (S/D 2011–2015). ARNE DAHL. P: SVT

Dortort, D. (USA 1959–1973). BONANZA National Broadcasting Company (NBC). 430 episodes.

Dreher, C. (2010). Auteur-Series — The Re-invention of Television. In C. Dreher (Ed.), (pp. 24–61). Stuttgart: Merz & Solitude.

Dreher, C. (Ed.) (2014). *Autorenserien II/Auteur Series II: Quality TV in den USA und Europa/Quality TV in USA and Europe*. Paderborn: Fink, Wilhelm.

Dreher, C., & Akass, K. (Eds.) (2010). *Autorenserien: Die Neuerfindung des Fernsehens*. Stuttgart: Merz & Solitude.

Dreher, C. & Lang, C. (2015). *Breaking Bad Breaking Down. Dramaturgie und Ästhetik einer Fernsehserie*. Wilhelm Fink: Paderborn.

Duchamp, Marcel. 2007 (1957). *The Creative Act*. Sub rosa.

Eco, U. (1990 (1977)). *Das offene Kunstwerk*. Frankfurt am Main: Suhrkamp Taschenbuch Verlag.

Eggeling, V. (D 1924). SYMPHONIE DIAGONALE.

Egri, L. (2004). *The art of dramatic writing: its basis in the creative interpretation of human motives*. London: Touchstone.

Eisenstein, S. (1951). *Film form: essays in film theory*: Dobson.

Eisenstein, S. (2001). Dramaturgie der Film Form (1929). In F.-J. Albersmeier (Ed.), *Texte zur Theorie des Films* (pp. 275–304). Leipzig: Philipp Reclam jr.

Eisenstein, Sergej M. 2006 "Die Vertikalmontage (1940–41)." In *Jenseits der Einstellung: Schriften zur Filmtheorie / Sergej M. Eisenstein.*, edited by Felix Lenz and Helmut H. Diedrichs, 238–300. Frankfurt am Main: Suhrkamp.

Eisenstein, S. (USSR 1944/58). ИВАН ГРОЗНЫЙ [IVAN THE TERRIBLE].

Eisler, H. (1947). *Composing for the films*. New York,: Oxford Univ. Press.

Eisler, H., (1975). Gespräche mit Hans Bunge.: Fragen Sie mehr über Brecht Gesammelte Werke. In (Fotomech. Nachdr. d. 1. Aufl. ed., pp. 433 S.).

Eisner, L. H. (2008). *The haunted screen; expressionism in the German cinema and the influence of Max Reinhardt [by] Lotte H. Eisner*. Berkeley and Los Angeles: Berkeley, University of California Press [1969].

Elsaesser, T. (2000). *Weimar cinema and after: Germany's historical imaginary*. London: Routledge.

Emmerich, R. (USA 1996). INDEPENDENCE DAY.

Emmerich, R. (USA 2004). THE DAY AFTER TOMORROW.

Enyedi, I. (H/D/CUB 1989). AZ ÉN XX. SZÁZADOM [MY TWENTIETH CENTURY]

Eschenbach, W. v. (1994). Parzival. In *Bibliothek deutscher Klassiker*. Frankfurt am Main: Dt. Klassiker-Verl.

Fellini, F. (I 1953). I VITELLONI

Fellini, F. (I 1954). LA STRADA.

Fellini, F. (I 1965). GIULIETTA DEGLI SPIRITI

Fiebach, J. (2002). Theatricality: From Oral Traditions to Televised "Realities". *SubStance, 31, Number 2&3*(98/99), 17–41.

Fiebach, J. (2006). *Gewordene Eigenart Theater, Medien, Kulturelle Kommunikation an der Humboldt-Universit©Pt zu Berlin*. Berlin: Vistas Verl.

Fiebach, J. (2015). *Welt Theater Geschichte. Eine Kulturgeschichte des Theatralen*. Berlin: Theater der Zeit.

Fiedler, L. A. (2017). *Love and death in the American novel* (3rd printing Dalkey Archive ed.). Normal, IL: Dalkey Archive Press.

Fleming, V. (USA 1939a). GONE WITH THE WIND.

Fleming, V. (USA 1939b). THE WIZARD OF OZ.

Ford, J. (1939). STAGECOACH.

Forman, M. (USA/F 1984). AMADEUS.

Freilich, S. (1964). драматургия экрана Film Dramaturgy. Berlin Henschel Verlag Berlin.

Frenz, H. (Ed.) (1962). Amerikanische Dramaturgie. Reinbek bei Hamburg: Rowohlt Verlag.

Freska, F. (o.J.). Sumurun.

Freyberger, Hans (Verfasser), and Jakob (Mitwirkender) Vonderlinn. 1913. Zentral-Perspektive. Leipzig: Göschen.

Freytag, G. Technique of the drama; an exposition of dramatic composition and art. An authorized translation from the 6th German ed. by Elias J. MacEwan: New York.

Friedel, H. & Hoberg, A. (2013) The Blue Rider in the Lenbachhaus, Munich.

Gaghan, S. (USA/VAE 2005). SYRIANA.

Garcia, R. (USA 2005). NINE LIVES.

Gatiss, M., Moffat, S., & Thompson, S. (2010–2017). SHERLOCK. P: BBC.

Gelfert, Hans-Dieter. 2006. Typisch amerikanisch: Wie die Amerikaner wurden, was sie sind. 3., aktualisierte und um ein Nachwort Amerika 2006 erg. Aufl., Originalausg. ed. München: Beck.

Genette, G. (2010). Die Erzählung. Paderborn: Fink.

German, A. (RU/PL/SRB 2018). ДОВЛАТОВ [DOVLATOV].

Gibson, M. (USA 2004). THE PASSION OF THE CHRIST.

Gilligan, V. (2008–2013). BREAKING BAD. P: HBO.

Girshausen, T. (2005). Mimesis. In E. Fischer-Lichte, D. Kolesch, & M. Warstat (Eds.), Metzler Lexikon Theatertheorie (pp. 201–208). Stuttgart: Metzler.

Grieg, E. (1997). In the hall of the mountain king: from the Peer Gynt suite for orchestra. Tewkesbury: Goodmusic Publishing, 2010.

Griffith, D. W. (USA 1915). BIRTH OF A NATION.

Griffith, D. W. (USA 1916). INTOLERANCE.

Gunther, I. (1995). Magic Realism, New Objectivity, and the Arts during the Weimar Republic. In L. P. Zamora & W. B. Faris (Eds.), Magical *realism: theory, history, community* (pp. 33–74). Durham & London: Dirham University Press.

Gusner, I. (2018). *Start in Moskau. Regiestudenten der Moskauer Filmhochschule erinnern sich*. Berlin: DEFA Stiftung.

Guthrie, W. K. C., & Warren, J. (2013). *The Greek philosophers from Thales to Aristotle*. Abingdon, Oxon: Routledge.

Guzmán, P. (F/Ch/E 2015). EL BOTÓN DE NÁCAR - [The Pearl Button].

Hahn, J. S., & Hahn, J. S. (1996). *Bible basics: an introduction & reference guide to the five books of Moses* (Hahn family ed.). Boca Raton, Fla.

Nanuet, NY: International Traditions Corp.Distribution by Feldheim Publishers.

Hammer, K. (Ed.) (1968). *Dramaturgische Schriften des 18. Jahrhunderts*. Berlin: Henschelverlag Berlin.

Hammer, K. (Ed.) (1987). *Dramaturgische Schriften des 19. Jahrhunderts*. Berlin: Henschel Verlag.

Hanalis, B. (USA 1974–1983). LITTLE HOUSE ON THE PRAIRIE. P: NBC

Hanson, Hart. (USA 2005–2017). BONES.

Hapkemeyer, A., & Hirschfeld-Mack, L. (2000). *Ludwig Hirschfeld-Mack: Bauhäusler und Visionär; [Museion, Museum für Moderne Kunst, Bozen, 17.3.–28.5.2000 …]*. Ostfildern-Ruit: Hatje Cantz.

Harrison, A. (1989). *Challenging De Gaulle: the O.A.S. and the counterrevolution in Algeria, 1954–1962*. New York: Praeger.

Hasche, C., Kalisch, E., & Weber, t. (Eds.). (2014). *Der dramaturgische Blick: Potenziale und Modelle von Dramaturgie im Medienwandel*. Berlin: Avinius Verlag.

Hašek, J. (1973). *The good soldier Svejk and his fortunes in the World War*. London,: Heinemann.

Hecht, W. (Ed.) (1979). *Brecht im Gespräch*. Berlin: Henschel Verlag.

Hegel, G. W. F. (1971). *Vorlesungen über die Ästhetik I/II*. Stuttgart: Reclam.

Hegel, G. W. F. (2003). *Die Poesie* ([Nachdr.] ed.). Stuttgart: Reclam.

Heller, Bruno. (USA 2008–2015). THE MENTALIST.

Herman, M. (UK 1996). BRASSED OFF.

Herschel, A. J. (1951). *The Sabbath.* New York: Farrar, Strauss and Giroux.

Hevesy, I. (1925). *A filmjáték esztétikája és dramaturgiája [Aesthetics and Dramaturgy of the Film Play].* Budapest, Hungary: Athenaeum.

Highsmith, P. (1957). *The Talented Mr. Ripley.* London: Cresset Press.

Hirschfeld-Mack, L. (1923). Farben-Licht-Spiele. In. Weimar: Bauhaus Dessau.

Holland, A. (D / PL / F 1990). EUROPA, EUROPA [OT: HITLERJUNGE SALOMON].

Homer. (8. Jh. v.u.Z). Die Odyssee - ἡ Ὀδύσσεια - hē Odýsseia.

Hopper, D. (USA 1969). EASY RIDER.

Hornby, R. (1986). *Drama, Metadrama and perception.* Lewisburg, Pa.: Bucknell University Press.

Huo, H.-h. (TWN/CHN/HKG 2015). 刺客聶隱娘 [THE ASSASSIN]
Ibsen, H., & Archer. (1927). *Rosmersholm: the Lady from the sea.* [S.l.]: William Heinemann ltd.

Iñárritu, A. G. (F/USA/MEX 2006). BABEL.

Jacobs, D. (USA 1978–1991). DALLAS.

Janser, A., Rüegg, A., Richter, H., & Richter, H. (2001). *Hans Richter: Die neue Wohnung: Architektur, Film, Raum.* Baden/Switzerland: Müller.

Jarmusch, J. (Writer). (USA/F/G 2016). Paterson In K. International, A. Studios, & I. Productions (Producer).

Kahneman, D. (2012). *Thinking, Fast And Slow.* London: Penguin Books.

Kant, I. (1974). *Kritik der Urteilskraft* Frankfurt/Main: Suhrkamp.

Kant, I. (1990). *The critique of pure reason; The critique of practical reason: and other ethical treatises; The critique of judgement.* Chicago; London: Encyclopaedia Britannica.

Kant, I. (2012). *Groundwork of the metaphysics of morals* (M. J. Gregor & J. Timmermann Eds. Rev. ed. / translation revised by Jens Timmermann. ed.). Cambridge: Cambridge University Press.

Kapur, S. (UK 1998). ELISABETH.

Kazan, E. (USA 1976). THE LAST TYCOON.

Khlebnikov, B., & Popogrebsky, A. (R 2003). КОКТЕБЕЛЬ [ROADS TO KOKTEBEL].

Kieślowski, K. (PL 1987 (1981)). PRZYPADEK

Kindermann, H. (1965). *Theatergeschichte Europas VII.Band: Realismus* (Vol. VII). Salzburg: O. Müller.

Klimow, E. G. (USSR 1985). IDI I SMOTRI [COME AND SEE].

Klotz, V. (1980). *Geschlossene und offene Form im Drama (1969)* (13 ed.). München: C. Hanser.

Kuba, A. (2005). Geste/Gestus. In E. Fischer-Lichte, D. Kolesch, & M. Warstadt (Eds.), *Metzler Lexikon Theatertheorie* (pp. 129–136). Stuttgart / Weimar: Verlag J.B. Metzler.

Kubrick, S. (UK/USA 1968). 2001 - A SPACE ODYSSEY. P: M.-G.-M. (MGM) & S.-K.-. Productions

Kubrick, S.. (UK/USA 1980). THE SHINING. P: CMS.

Kurosawa, A. (J 1950). 羅生門 [RASHÔMON].

Kurosawa, A. (J 1990). 夢 [DREAMS].

Kurzel, J. (UK/F/USA 2015). MACBETH.

Larrain, P. (USA/CHI/F/D 2016). JACKY.

Lavery, D. (2010). The Imagination Will Be Televised: Showrunning and the Re-animation of Authorship in the 21st Century American Television. In C. Dreher (Ed.), *Auteur-Series - The Re-invention of Television I* (Vol. i, pp. 64–71). Stuttgart: Merz & Solitude.

Lean, D. (UK 1950). MADELEINE.

Lean, D. (UK 1962). LAWRENCE OF ARABIA.

Lee, A. (USA 1997). THE ICE STORM.

Lee, S. (USA 2006). INSIDE MAN.

Lefèbvre, H. Über Charlie Chaplin, Bertolt Brecht und einige andere. In D. Kimmich (Ed.), *Charlie Chapin. Eine Ikone der Moderne.* (pp. 236). Frankfurt am Main: Suhrkamp Verlag.

Lessing, G. E. (2012). *Laokoon, oder, Über die Grenzen der Malerei und Poesie: Studienausgabe*. Stuttgart: Reclam.

Lessing, G. E., & Berghahn, K. L. (1981). *Hamburgische Dramaturgie (1925)*. Stuttgart: Reclam.

Lessing, G. E., & Frothingham, E. (1874). *Laocoon. An essay upon the limits of painting and poetry*. Boston,: Roberts brothers.

Lessing, G. E., & Machaffie, M. A. (1962). *Minna von Barnhelm. Edited by Margaret A. McHaffie*. London; Edinburgh: Thomas Nelson & Sons.

Lessing, G. E., & Riemann, R. (1899). *Minna von Barnhelm. Miß Sara Sampson* [u.a.]. Werke. In (pp. 352 S.).

Lessing, G. E., & Stahl, E. L. (1946). *Emilia Galotti. Edited by E. L. Stahl*: Oxford.

Lessing, G. E., & Zimmern, H. (1962). *Hamburg Dramaturgy*. N.Y.: Dover.

Liss, H., Boeckler, A. M., & Landthaler, B. (2011). *TANACH Lehrbuch der juedischen Bibel* (3., unver. Aufl. ed.). Heidelberg: Winter.

Liss, H., Bœckler, A. M., & Landthaler, B. (2011). *TANACH. Lehrbuch der jüdischen Bibel* (3., unver. Aufl. ed.). Heidelberg: Winter.

Loteanu, E. (USSR 1977). ТАБОР УХОДИТ В НЕБО [QUEEN OF THE GYPSIES].

Lotman, J. M. (1977). *Probleme der Kinoästhetik (Semiotika kino i problem kinoestetiki, dt.): Einführung in die Semiotik des Films*. Frankfurt a.M: Syndikat.

Lotman, J. M. (1981a). Das Sujet im Film. In *Kunst als Sprache. Untersuchungen zum Zeichencharakter von Literatur und Kunst* (pp. 205–218). Leipzig: Verlag Philipp Reclam jun.

Lotman, J. M. (1981b). Die Entstehung des Sujets - typologisch gesehen. In K. Städtke (Ed.), *Lotman, Juri M.: Kunst als Sprache*. (pp. 175–205). Leipzig: Reclam.

Lubitsch, E. (D 1920). SUMURUN.

Lubitsch, E. (USA 1939). NINOTCHKA.

Lucas, G. (USA 1977). STAR WARS.

Lumière, A., & Lumière, L. (F 1896). L'ARRIVÉE D'UN TRAIN EN GARE DE LA CIOTAT IN S. LUMIÈRE

Lynch, D. (USA 2001). MULHOLLAND DRIVE

Lynch, David. (USA 1980). TWIN PEAKS.

Maïwenn (F 2011). POLISSE.

Malkin, J. R., & Rokem, F. (2010). *Jews and the making of modern German theatre*. Iowa City: University of Iowa Press.

Malle, L. (F/D/I 1987). AU REVOIR LES ENFANTS.

Mamet, D. (1991). *On directing film*. London: Faber, 1992.

Mankell, H. (S/D/DK/N/FIN 2005–2013). WALLANDER.

Mann, M. (USA 1984–1990). MIAMI VICE.

Mann, M. (USA 2004). COLLATERAL.

Martínez, M., & Scheffel, M. (2007). *Einführung in die Erzähltheorie* (7 ed.). Müchen: C.H. Beck.

Matt, P. v. (2002). *Liebesverrat: Die Treulosen in der Literatur* ([Nachdr.] ed.). München [u.a.]: Hanser.

Matt, P. v. (2006). *Die Intrige: Theorie und Praxis der Hinterlist*. München: C. Hanser.

Maurer, R., & Jarmusch, J. (2006). *Jim Jarmusch Filme zum anderen Amerika*. Mainz: Bender.

Maxwell, Robert. (USA 1954–1973.) LASSIE.

McDonald, B. (CDN 2007). THE TRACEY FRAGMENTS

Mehta, D. ((1998). IND/CDN EARTH.

Mehta, D. (CAN/IND 2005). WATER.

Mertes, R. (I/G/USA 1999). ESTHER.

Metamorphoseon libri XI [The Golden Ass]. (2. cent.). Ostia.

Metschler, T. (2010). Das Mimesisprinzip vom ausgehenden 18. Jahrhundert zur Moderne: Nicht >Ende einer Denkform<, sondern ihre Transformation. In K. Barck (Ed.), *Ästhetische Grundbegriffe: Historisches Wörterbuch in sieben Bänden* (Studienausgabe. ed., Vol. 6, pp. 644–662). Stuttgart: Metzler.

Mettler, P. (CDN/CH 2012). THE END OF TIME.

Michalski, S. (1994). *New objectivity: painting, graphic art and photography in Weimar Germany, 1919–1933*. Köln: Benedikt Taschen.

Miller, A. (1958). The Shadow of the Gods. *Harper's Magazin*(August).

Minghella, A. (USA/UK 1996). THE ENGLISH PATIENT. P: Miramax & T. M. Production

Minghella, A., & Highsmith, P. T. M. R. *The talented Mr. Ripley: a screenplay*.

Mnouchkine, A. (F 1974). 1789.

Mnouchkine, A. (F 1978). MOLIÈRE.

Moholy-Nagy, L. (1925). *Malerei, Photographie, Film*. München: Langen.

Moholy-Nagy, L. (1967). *Painting. Photography. Film* (J. Seligman, Trans. H. M. Wingler Ed.). London: Lund Humphries.

Müller, T. (1927). Hoppla, wir leben! (Bühnenbild-Entwürfe). Retrieved 19 August 2018, from Institut für Theaterwissenschaft der Freien Universität Berlin, Theaterhistorische Sammlungen https://wikis.fu-berlin.de/pages/viewpage.action?pageId=722044306

Murasaki, S., & Tyler, R. (2001). *The tale of Genji*. New York; London: Penguin, 2003.

Murch, W. (2001). *In the blink of an eye: A perspective on film editing* (2nd ed ed.). Los Angeles: Silman-James Press.

Murnau, F. W. (D 1922). NOSFERATU, EINE SYMPHONIE DES GRAUENS.

Murnau, F. W. (USA 1927). SUNRISE: A SONG OF TWO HUMANS

Murnau, F. W. (USA 1931). TABU: A STORY OF THE SOUTH SEAS

n.n. (2011). 'Agfa' according to those who lived it. *Haaretz*. Retrieved from https://www.haaretz.com/1.5222251/1.5222251

Nagler, A. M. (1959). *A source book in theatrical history = Sources of theatrical history*. New York: Dover Publications.

o.N. (1867, Oktober 1867). Der Indianerkrieg. *Calwer Missionsblatt: Eine allg. Ill. Missionszeitschrift*, p. 10/11.

Olmi, E., Kiarostami, A., & Loach, K. (I/UK 2005). TICKETS.

Ondaatje, M., & Murch, W. (2002). *The conversations: Walter Murch and the art of editing film*. Toronto: Vintage Canada.

Pabst, G. (D 1926). GEHEIMNISSE EINER SEELE [SECRETS OF A SOUL].

Parajanov, S. (USSR 1969). Նռան գույնը [THE COLOR OF POMEGRANATES].

Paramount (2006 25 July 2018). BABEL - Trailer (HD). Retrieved from https://www.youtube.com/watch?v=JCJ2zIgZFgU

Parker, A. (USA 1996). EVITA.

Pearlman, K. (2009). *Cutting rhythms: Shaping the film edit*. Amsterdam; Boston: Focal Press/Elsevier.

Peckinpah, S. (USA 1969). THE WILD BUNCH.

Pesic, P. (2017). *Polyphonic minds: music, science, and expression* (e-book ed.). Cambridge, MA: The MIT Press.

Petersen, W. (USA 2000). THE PERFECT STORM

Pichler, B., & Pollach, A. (Eds.). (2006). *moving landscapes - Landschaft und Film*. Wien: Synema.

Polański, R. (UK/F/D 2010). THE GHOST WRITER [DVD].

Pollack, S. (USA/UK 1985). OUT OF AFRICA.

Porter, E. S. (USA 1903). THE GREAT TRAIN ROBBERY

Portis, C. (1968). *True Grit*. USA Simon & Schuster.

Potter, G. (2015, 2016). Dramaturgy and Film. In M. Romanska (Ed.), *The Routledge Companion to Dramaturgy* (pp. 359–363). Oxon, New York: Routledge.

Potter, S. (UK/R/I/F/NL 1992). ORLANDO.

Raff, Gideon. 2009–2012. HATUFIM. IRS: Keshet TV

Rancière, J. (2011). *The emancipated spectator*. London: Verso.

Raskin, R. (2002). *The art of the short fiction film: a shot by shot study of nine modern classics*. Jefferson, N.C.; London: McFarland.

Redvall, E. N. (2013). *Writing and producing television drama in Denmark: From The Kingdom to The Killing*.

Reinhardt, M. (D 1910). SUMURÛN.

Resnais, A. (F 1959). HIROSHIMA MON AMOUR.

Roddenberry, G. (USA 1966–1969). STAR TREK.

Rohmer, R. (2000). 'implizite' oder 'versteckte' Dramaturgien.: Skizzierung eines wandelbaren Phänomens - Hypothesen zu seiner theaterhistorischen und theatertheoretischen Bestimmung. In P. Reichel (Ed.), *Studien zur Dramaturgie* (pp. 13–24). Tübingen: Narr.

Romanska, M. (2015). *The Routledge companion to dramaturgy*. London; New York: Routledge.

Romanska, M. (2016). Introduction. In M. Romanska (Ed.), *The Routledge Companion to Dramaturgy* (pp. 1–16). Oxon/New York: Routledge.

Romm, M. (1980). *Избранных произведений* (Vol. 3). Moscow: Искусство.

Romm, M. I. i. (1974). Dramaturgie heute: Vorlesung gehalten vor den höheren Szenaristenkursen 1962 im Mosfilmstudio *Theorie und Praxis des Films*, 3, 8.

Romm, M. I. i. (1980). *Избранных произведений* (Vol. 3). Moscow: Искусство.

Rosenfeldt, Hans. S/Dk 2012–2018. Bron | Broen [The Bridge].

Röttgers, K., & Schmitz-Emans, M. (Eds.). (1999). *Perspektive in Literatur und bildender Kunst*. Essen: Verl. Die Blaue Eule.

Rühle, G. (1988). Das Theater der Republik. In G. Rühle (Ed.), *Theater für die Republik - Im Spiegel der Kritik* (Vol. 1. 1917–1933, pp. 11–45). Berlin: Henschel Verlag.

Ruttmann, W. (D 1921–1925). OPUS I - IV.

Sachs, H., Badstübner, E., & Neumann, H. (1980). *Christliche Ikonographie in Stichworten* (2. verbesserte ed.). Leipzig: Koehler & Amelang.

Samosata, L. o. (180). *A True Story*.

Scaliger, J. C., Deitz, L., & Vogt-Spira, G. *Poetices libri septem*. Stuttgart-Bad Cannstatt: Frommann-Holzboog.

Schafer, R. M. (1993). *The Soundscape. In Our Sonic Environment and the Tuning of the World*. (pp. 320 pages / 6446kb).

Schechner, R. *Performance theory* (Rev. and expanded ed. ed.): London: Routledge, 2003 (2005 printing).

Schmitt, A. (2008a). Kommentar. In Aristoteles & A. Schmitt (Eds.), *Aristoteles: Poetik. Übersetzt und erläutert von Arbogast Schmitt* (pp. 193–742). Berlin: Akad.-Verl.

Schmitt, A. (2008b). Vorwort. In Aristoteles & A. Schmitt (Eds.), *Aristoteles: Poetik. Übersetzt und erläutert von Arbogast Schmitt* (pp. I–XIV). Berlin: Akademie-Verlag.

Scorsese, M. (USA 2010). SHUTTER ISLAND.

Seesslen, G. (1982). *Klassiker der Filmkomik Geschichte und Mythologie des komischen Films*. Reinbek b. Hamburg: Rowohlt.

Shakespeare, W. (1962). *The Complete Works of William Shakespeare*. London, New York, Toronto: Oxford University Press.

Shakespeare, W. (n.y.-a). Hamlet. In (pp. 945–980). London: Spring Books.

Shakespeare, W. (n.y.-b). A Midsummer Night's Dream In (pp. 139–157). London: Spring Books.

Shakespeare, W. (n.y.-c). The Taming of the Shrew (1590–1592). In (pp. 261–286). London: Spring Books.

Shapiro, E., & Shapiro, R. A. (USA 1981–1989). DYNASTY

Sherman-Palladino, Amy. USA 2017-. THE MARVELOUS MRS. MAISEL.

Simon, R. (GDR 1980). JADUP UND BOEL [JADUP AND BOEL].

Singer, B. (USA/G 1995). THE USUAL SUSPECTS.

Simon, David. (USA 2002–2008). THE WIRE

Siodmak, R., Ulmer, E. G., Gliese, R., Siodmak, C., & Zinnemann, F. (D 1930). MENSCHEN AM SONNTAG [PEOPLE ON SUNDAY].

Sklovskij, V. (2005). Das Sujet in der Filmkunst (1923). In W. Beilenhoff (Ed.), *Poetika Kino* (Vol. stw 1733, pp. 221–230). Frankfurt am Main: suhrkamp

Smith, J. D. (2009). *The Mahābhārata*. London: Penguin.

Soderbergh, S. (USA 2000). ERIN BROCKOVICH.

Spingarn, J. E. (1899). *A History of Literary Criticism in the Renaissance. With special reference to the influence of Italy in the formation and development of modern classicism.*

Statistica. (2018). Employment in coal mining industry in the United Kingdom (UK) 1920–2017. https://www.statista.com/statistics/371069/employment-in-coal-mining-industry-in-the-united-kingdom-uk/

Staudte, W. (1949). ROTATION. P: DEFA

Stein, G. (1935). *Narration*. Chicago: University of Chicago Press.

Stein, G., & Wilder, T. (2010). *Narration: four lectures*. Chicago; London: The University of Chicago Press.

Stroheim, E. v. (USA 1924). GREED.

Stutterheim, K. (2010). Fiktionalisierte Wirklichkeiten. Dokudrama und Realfiction-Filme als Grenzgänger im deutschen Fernsehen. In A. Bartl & S. Catani (Eds.), *Bastard. Figurationen des Hybriden zwischen Ausgrenzung und Entgrenzung* (pp. 239–254). Würzburg: Könighausen & Neumann.

Stutterheim, K. (2013a). Hitchcock's Spellbound - wie Alfred Hitchcock von der dramatischen Struktur ablenkt. Retrieved from http://www. kino-glaz.de/archives/486

Stutterheim, K. (2013b). Postmoderne - Eine Annäherung an eine Definition. In K. Stutterheim & C. Lang (Eds.), *"Come and play with us"* (pp. 13–38). Marburg: Schüren.

Stutterheim, K. (2013c). Shutter Island: Dialogizität, Imagination und implizite Dramaturgie. In H.-P. Preusser (Ed.), *Anschauen und Vorstellen* (pp. 116–131). Marburg: Schüren.

Stutterheim, K. (2013d). Überlegungen zur Ästhetik des postmodernen Films. In K. Stutterheim & C. Lang (Eds.), *"Come and play with us"* (pp. 39–87). Marburg: Schüren.

Stutterheim, K. (2014a). Filmdramaturgie als ‚Geheimnis des Erzählens'. In *Der dramaturgische Blick*. Berlin: Avinius Verlag.

Stutterheim, K. (2014b). Häutungen eines Genres - skandinavische Ermittlerinnen Generic Metamorphosis – Scandinavian Investigators. In C. Dreher (Ed.), *Autorenserien II / Auteur Series II* (pp. 171–219). Paderborn: Fink, Wilhelm.

Stutterheim, K. (2015). *Handbuch angewandter Dramaturgie. Vom Geheimnis des filmischen Erzählens*. Frankfurt am Main u.a.: Peter Lang Verlag.

Stutterheim, K. (2016). Why the audience is not the measurement. from kino-glaz

Stutterheim, K. (2017). *Game of Thrones sehen - Dramaturgie einer TV Serie*. Paderborn Fink Verlag / Brill

Stutterheim, K. (2020). *Dramaturgy for Film and TV*. London & New York Routledge.

Stutterheim, K., & Kaiser, S. (2011). *Handbuch der Filmdramaturgie: Das Bauchgefühl und seine Ursachen* (2te überarbeitete Ausgabe ed.). Frankfurt am Main: Peter Lang Verlag.

Stutterheim, K., & Lang, C. (Eds.). (2013). *"Come and play with us": Dramaturgie und Ästhetik im postmodernen Kino*. Marburg: Schüren.

Sound of Cinema (2018, 16 June 2018). [Retrieved from https://www.bbc.co.uk/radio/play/b0b65mrf

Sveistrup, Søren. 2007–2012. FORBYDELSEN. DK/N/S/D.

Szekfü, A. (2018). Iván Hevesy and the Revolution of the Second Plan. *Cinema Journal, 57*(3), 22.

Szondi, P. (1965). *Theorie des modernen Dramas (1880–1950)* (Vol. 27). Frankfurt a.M: Suhrkamp Verlag.

Szondi, P. (1987). *Theory of the modern drama: a critical edition.* Minneapolis: University of Minnesota Press.

Tarkovsky, A. (I/USSR 1983). Ностальгия Nostalghia. In R. 2 & Sovinfilm (Producer).

Tarkovskii, A. a., & Hunter-Blair, K. w. o. s. t. c. t. c. *Poetry and film: artistic kinship between Arsenii and Andrei Tarkovsky.*

Tarkovsky, A. (1986). *Sculpting in Time* (K. Hunter-Blair, Trans.). London: The Bodley Head.

Tarkovsky, A. (USSR 1961). ИВАНОВО ДЕТСТВО - [IVAN'S CHILDHOOD]

Tarkovsky, A. (USSR 1979). STALKER.

Träger, C. (Ed.) (1986). *Wörterbuch der Literaturwissenschaft* (1 ed.). Leipzig: Bibliogr. Inst.

Truffaut, F., Grafe, F., & Patalas, E. (2007). *Mr. Hitchcock, wie haben Sie das gemacht? (Le cinéma selon Hitchcock, dt.- Übers. v. Frieda Grafe u. Enno Patalas. Ungekürzte Taschenbuchausg.)* (4. ed.). München: Heyne.

Tucker, A. (UK 1998). HILARY & JACKIE.

Turin, V. A. (USSR 1929). TURKSIB (Туркестано-Сибирская железная дорога, Турксиб).

Turner, C., & Behrndt, S. K. (2016). *dramaturgy and performance* (Revised edition. ed.): macmillen education palgrave

ТУРКИН, В. К., & (Turkin, V. K. ((1938) 2007). *драматургія кинó.* . Moscow: ВГИК.

Tykwer, T. (D 1998). LOLA RENNT.

Tynjanov, J. (2005). Über Sujet und Fabel im Film (1926). In W. Beilenhoff (Ed.), *Poetika Kino* (pp. 466). Frankfurt am Main: Suhrkamp.

Viertel, B. (D/USA 1926). ABENTEUER EINES ZEHNMARKSCHEINES [Adventures of a Ten Mark Note]

Vinken, B. (2013). *Angezogen: Das Geheimnis der Mode*. Stuttgart: Klett-Cotta.

Wachowsi&Wachowski (Writer). (USA 1999). THE MATRIX.

Wainwright, S. (UK 2014 -). HAPPY VALLEY

Wainwright, S., & Taylor, D. (Writers). (UK 2011–2016)). SCOTT & BAILEY. In.

Waisfeld, I. (1966). мастерство кинодраматургия [*Dramaturgy of the Movies*]. Berlin Henschel Verlag Berlin.

Warnke, M. (1992). *Politische Landschaft: zur Kunstgeschichte der Natur*. München u.a.: Hanser.

Warren, T. ((UK 1960-). CORONATION STREET.

Watt, H., & Wright, B. (UK 1936). NIGHT MAIL.

Wegener, P. (D 1920). DER GOLEM, WIE ER IN DIE WELT KAM.

Welles, O. (USA 1941). CITIZEN KANE.

Wiene, R. (D 1920). DAS CABINET DES DOKTOR CALIGARI.

Willett, J. (1978). *The theatre of Erwin Piscator: half a century of politics in the theatre*. London: Eyre Methuen, 1986.

Willig, Th. A. 1894. *Taschenbuch für Zeichenlehrer*. Breslau: Ferdinant Hirt, Königliche Universitäts- und Verlagsbuchhandlung.

Wolf, K. (GDR 1959). STERNE [STARS].

Wolf, K. (GDR 1971). GOYA - ODER DER ARGE WEG DER ERKENNTNIS.

Wyler, W. (USA 1959). BEN HUR.

Zemeckis, R. (USA 1997). CONTACT.

Zemeckis, R. (USA 2000). CAST AWAY.

Zhangke, J. (CH 2006). STILL LIFE[三峡好人 - San Xia Hao Ren]

Zinnemann, F. (UK/F 1973). THE DAY OF THE JACKAL. J. W. Productions, W. F. Productions, & U. Productions.

Zuicker, Anthony E. (USA 2000–2015). CSI: CRIME SCENE INVESTIGATION.

Index